BRECKENRIDGE

150 Years of Golden History

Mary Ellen Gilliland

 Alpenrose Press

Library of Congress Control Number: 2009902854

ISBN: 978-1-889385-11-2

Other local books by Mary Ellen Gilliland:
> SUMMIT, A Gold Rush History of Summit County, Colorado
> > *25th Anniversary Edition*
> The New Summit Hiker
> The Vail Hiker
> Frisco, A Colorful Colorado Community
> Seasons in the Sun
> Lula, Portrait In Pictures and Prose
> > *of a Keystone, Colorado Family*
> A Century of Faith
> Heaven On Earth, Here And Now
> Colorado Rascals, Scoundrels and No Goods
> > *of Breckenridge, Frisco, Dillon, Keystone and Silverthorne*

Visit Our Web Site, **www.alpenrosepress.com**
for more history, antique photographs, historic hikes
and ski or snowshoe trails and author comments.

To Order Books: www.alpenrosepress.com/APOrderBlank.htm

 Alpenrose Press

Box 499
Silverthorne, Colorado 80498
(970) 468-6273
orders@alpenrosepress.com

Contents

Introduction

In Spring 2008 I re-read an eye-witness account of the 1859 Colorado gold rush. For the first time, I noticed a small but significant fact. The writer related that he arrived in the Blue River Diggings, today's Breckenridge, in late May, 1859. This May date disputes the accepted August, 1859 prospector influx date. Intense research turned up other early arrivals. I then began to question the traditional version of our local gold rush, mainly drawn from 1890s historian, Frank Hall, who interviewed Ruben Spaulding of first-gold-strike fame. Soon I discovered more ground-breaking facts that shed a new and different light on travel over the high passes and the whole story of Breckenridge 150 years ago in 1859. Enjoy!

Acknowledgments

I gratefully acknowledge the help of Larry Gilliland, Bill Fountain, Maureen Nicholls, Larissa Enns, Jim Yust, Roxie Knudsen, Cynthia Anderson, Rick Hague, David Spencer, Ed Bathke, Rich Skovlin, Gary Miller, Robin Theobald, Terry Perkins, Virginia Kloberdanz, Chick Deming and Wendy Wolfe. Special warm thanks to my editor, Sheliah Reynolds of Resonate Communications in Denver.

Mary Ellen Gilliland

1

Imagine 1859

T he land lay waiting. Pristine and untrammeled, the Blue River Valley hosted only abundant game—grizzly and brown bear, bighorn sheep, raptors, songbirds, elk, deer, fox, mountain lion, streams flashing trout—and its native people, the nomadic Ute Indians. Then, on August 10, 1859, a miner named Ruben J. Spaulding struck gold on a sandbar in the Blue River, the first gold discovery west of the Divide. His cry of "Eureka" rang against the walls of the Continental Divide and caused thousands of prospectors to scramble over the cordillera they called "the Snowy Range." The town that sprang up to house this horde became Breckenridge, the first town on Colorado's Western Slope.

These words introduced many of my historic speaker presentations and formed the bedrock of many of my historical books and articles. Other historians told the same story. However, my research for this book, done for Breckenridge's 150th anniversary, yielded historical nuggets which enrich our cache of knowledge and refine the old story into a glistening new tale.

The new discoveries advance understanding of the rich history of Breckenridge. This log and shanty 1860 mine camp matured into a Victorian architectural gem in the 1880s. One hundred and fifty years later it celebrates a new identity as a charming and historic Colorado ski and summer fun destination. Always, the golden strand of mining's history links the town to its 1859 beginnings.

Did the land wait in tranquil solitude for Ruben J. Spaulding's cry of "Eureka?"

No. The old story erred. The alpine beauty of the land the Utes called "Nahoonkara" already bustled with prospector activity when Spaulding's party of 14 descended Hoosier Pass to pan for gold on the Blue River in present-day Breckenridge. The first arrivals already named the area "The Blue River Diggings."

A wild crew of young and boisterous gold seekers had already riddled creek banks and stream beds searching for gold by the time Spaulding reached the Blue. Daniel Conner, for example, arrived May

23, 1859, more than six weeks ahead of Spaulding. Conner found active placer miners on the Blue. The reason he crossed the Snowy Range to reach the Blue: he had already heard of gold discoveries there in May, 1859. This he records in his book, *A Confederate in the Colorado Gold Fields*.

Felix Poznansky arrived in July, 1859. This fact appears in a manuscript the author recently discovered. Poznansky's personal essay reports that he found the Blue humming. Charles Runyon, who arrived in Denver in 1858, came to the Blue River on June 16, 1859. This information comes from an essay derived from personal interview done a century ago by student Ella Foote.

The combination of recently-discovered historical manuscripts, and the fact that Conner's information lies buried in his text, long obscured these facts from this writer until spring, 2008. I re-read Conner's book then and pieced the facts together.

For well over two months before Spaulding, the Blue River Diggings buzzed like a hive, with prospectors seeking placer gold. They surely found the gold flakes, gold dust and gold nuggets that drove them across half an untamed continent and over a snow-clogged 12,000-foot mountain ridge to unearth.

Evidence for pre-Spaulding Prospector Activity

1. Daniel Conner left Lawrence, Kansas on April 8, 1859. He reports in his *A Confederate in the Colorado Gold Fields* that he traveled 45 days to reach the Blue River Diggings. That puts his arrival at May 23, more than six weeks earlier than the Spaulding party, which didn't leave Denver until August 2, 1859.

2. Conner crossed the Continental Divide, despite heavy spring snowpack, because his party had picked up stories of gold strikes on the Blue River. He recounts the progress of travel from Pikes Peak to the site of a later town, Hamilton, saying "We were now eighty miles westerly of Pike's Peak and near where it was purported that gold had been found. It was on the other side of the cordillera, a distance of sixteen miles." Conner states that upon his arrival on the Blue, he found men already placer mining in Miners District in late May, 1859.

3. Charles Runyon, a Breckenridge old-timer, asserts in a published 1900s interview with student Ella Foote that his arrival date on the Blue was June 16, 1859.

4. Felix Poznansky's personal memoir, "Early History of Mining on the Blue River and Vicinity," records his arrival on the Blue as July, 1859, before Spaulding's party came in August.

Alpine Splendor

Along with gold gleaming in creek sands, these first arrivals found an alpine paradise unparalleled in beauty.

Mountain crags split by cascading waterfalls, rich green evergreen forests formed by huge primeval trees and soaring snow-crowned peaks greeted the gold rush travelers. The forests, alive with game, yielded easy rewards for hunters. Pure water rushed in roiling creeks with trout so abundant that pulling out 50 pounds of fish in fifteen minutes exhausted the fisherman's arm. The gold seekers tramped through mountain meadows dappled by dainty wildflowers in a glorious palette of color.

A precious few seemed to notice, and fewer possessed the verbal skills to capture this charm in words. But those who did wrote letters describing swaths of alpine grass stretching like green carpet to the top of the 12,000-foot Continental Divide, which they called the Snowy Range. They pictured granite pinnacles along the trail draped in churning mist. They reached the summit of the Divide to gape west at an endless panorama of successive snow-capped mountain ranges rippling across the vast horizon. Their words portrayed a paradise.

Like the Spaulding party later, the first arrivals began muddying those crystal streams with diversion projects. They felled ancient trees for mining lumber. They harvested wild game for meat. After all, the miners had come to mine. Most gave little observance to their natural surroundings—and less note in the early months to record keeping.

That's why Spaulding's strike stood so long as the first documented Blue River gold discovery. It prompted formation of a mining district, a legal entity borrowed from the 1849-born California gold rush. His find earned ranking as Discovery Claim in the new Spaulding Diggings, located one-fourth mile north of today's Main Street-Ski Hill Road intersection. Prospectors then filed adjacent claims both up and down river from "Discovery" under the legal jurisdiction of the district, formed August 15, 1859. Spaulding's party consisted of experienced miners, not raw youths off the farm or pale clerks from a city mercantile. These seasoned prospectors left behind a log book that is a treasure, Breckenridge's earliest mining record.

Its notations, in the elegant script so well-practiced in 1800s schoolhouses, included the claim of pioneer Will Iliff, who immediately panned $2 in pay dirt on the Blue's east bank, near Spaulding's strike. His placer site quickly yielded $7,000 in gold, a fortune in 1859. (Look for Will Iliff later in this book; unlike many, he remained in Breckenridge for decades after the initial gold rush.)

This writer is now sure that Spaulding's 14-member party missed being first on the scene.

Miners District

It's now clear that Spaulding's was not the first local mining district. Daniel Conner, an eye witness, relates in his book that in May, 1859 an initial organization, Miners District, had already formed. This district stretched from along the Blue River at the mouth of Indiana Gulch, south of today's Breckenridge. Though this mining district's book is lost, Conner's first-hand report establishes the existence of a mining district prior to Spaulding. Conner also declares that an unruly assortment of strangers had already created a commotion in the once-virgin valley:

> The first mining district ever organized in Summit County was called Miner's District, and laid across the waters of Blue River . . . We remained here for the time as a headquarters and busily prospected the surrounding country for a distance of twenty miles . . . Immigration now began to crowd Miners District with an unruly population . . . who immediately became savage on the question of the ownership of mining claims.

Until the mining district and especially the miners' court organized, claim jumping flourished. Conner said,

> A miner could hardly leave his pit long enough to get his dinner without finding someone in it at work with all the tools left there when he returned. This was called jumping claims. The result of this sort of conduct was that neighboring claim holders united in their protests . . . in an armed body . . . Lives were lost and conflicts inaugurated without limit. A body of tramps would unite and "jump" the whole district, drive out the original owners and pass new laws, and work until they would be served the same way.

Traveling journalist Henry Villard backs up Conner's statement in a book written about his 1859 visit to Colorado. In *The Past and Present of the Pike's Peak Gold Regions* he reported:

> The utter absence of all laws during the spring, summer and fall of 1859, together with the large number of desperadoes that always infest border and especially gold countries, caused a good deal of lawlessness . . . (perpetrated by) many individuals, that relied on their wits more than their muscles and sinews for a living.

Villard recognized that "muscles and sinews" proved a requirement for all who crossed the plains and clawed their way into the mountains. Those who possessed strength and stamina made it. They faced Indian hazards and danger on the trek across the Great Plains. Then they strained lugging packs on the steep ascent of the Snowy Range. It exhausted the unhardy. This is why many of those who first reached the

Blue were young men in their older teens and young twenties.

Spaulding and his party led by Charles Lawrence, and probably other groups as well, traveled to the Blue River Diggings "the long way," heading south from Denver on August 2, 1859 to today's Colorado Springs, then climbing to South Park toward today's Fairplay and over Hoosier Pass into the Blue River Diggings, a trip of 178 miles. (Their letters home called Hoosier by its early name "Ute Pass," because traveling Ute parties frequented the crossing.) But Daniel Conner and many more used another much shorter route, unknown till now. This shorter route, long shrouded in misinformation and long unrecognized, was the major gold rush route to the early Blue River Diggings.

Scaling the High Passes

The 1859 pioneers, burdened with back-breaking, joint-grinding loads of food, cooking utensils, bedding and mining equipment, labored their way over the Continental Divide via Tarryall Pass. Because the pass lay buried in snow in spring and early summer, the men had to abandon their wagons, if they had them, and post-hole through the snow on foot. Even those with mules spent precious hours attempting to extricate their loyal beasts from heavy, wet snow. Many gold seekers lamented the steepness of the final ascent over Tarryall Pass. Poor early-day record keeping has blurred the history of this main gold rush route and steered historians to believe that steep Tarryall Pass is the same crossing as the present-day, and much gentler, Boreas Pass.

Etching from Harpers Illustrated Weekly

Topping the Pass

Many Colorado historical books group the names of the passes, Tarryall, Hamilton and Breckenridge together, explaining that these were early names for the present-day Boreas Pass. Mounting evidence indicates that Tarryall, Hamilton and Breckenridge (now called Boreas) are three different passes. New information (see box) suggests that Tarryall Pass, located on the ridge southwest of today's Boreas Pass, served as the initial 1859 route. There the ten-mile-long Hoosier Ridge forms the

Divide as it connects Boreas Pass and Hoosier Pass to the southwest. Two saddles appear close to Boreas Pass along the ridge. One, located a half-mile above and southwest of Boreas, empties directly into Indiana Gulch, where an 1860s wagon road and an 1870s stagecoach route descended to meet the Blue River. This is Tarryall Pass; its altitude, 12,029 feet, agrees with the reports of early pass travelers. Another, larger and broader saddle, located further along the Divide about a mile southwest of today's Boreas, leads into both Indiana and Pennsylvania Gulches. This was Hamilton Pass, altitude 11,680 feet. An 1861 post road, "the Breckenridge Road," crossed here. Hamilton was also called Breckenridge Pass early on, which adds to the confusion.

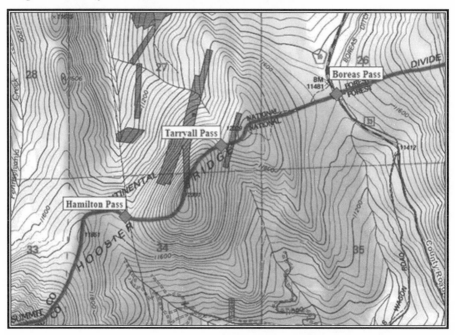

1859 miners scaled challenging 12,029-foot TarryallPass to cross the Snowy Range from Tarryall. By 1860 Hamilton Pass came into use.

An intriguing story emerges from the memoirs of Thomas Breckenridge, who reports he traveled in 1845 with explorer Colonel John C. Fremont, America's famous "Pathfinder." Breckenridge's memoir relates that he lost his mule and left his party to search. He crossed the Snowy Range to the Blue on the Hamilton Pass route where later gold seekers would cross the summit. Breckenridge expected to hunt an hour or so for the mule but frightened his companions when the search lasted two days. When he finally returned and re-crossed the ridge-spanning saddle, Fremont named it Breckenridge Pass ("for a stubborn mule," he said) to remind the shame-faced Breckenridge of his ill-conceived disappearance. (Some say the later town took its name from that same Breckenridge Pass.)

The first gold seekers probably used both Tarryall and Hamilton (initially called Breckenridge) passes to cross the Divide. However, an 1861 wagon road, the Bradford and Blue River toll road, selected a route that climbed toward Hamilton Pass, the gentler saddle at 11,680 feet. It offered an easier path for horse and foot travel. As soon as road builders constructed this rough road, most traffic—foot, horseback and wagon—shifted to that route. A rough road still crosses the Divide there today. Power lines mark the crossing. In 1866 when the new Hamilton and Breckinridge (sic) Road Company built its toll road, the route shifted to the present-day Boreas crossing. From 1867 on, this route adopted the Breckenridge Pass name and progressively increased in use.

Journalists and historians have employed the names Breckenridge Pass, Tarryall Pass, Hamilton Pass and Boreas Pass interchangeably. Confusing Tarryall Pass with Boreas and even Hamilton is easy because the two routes lie fairly close together on the ridge. And all three of them lead to Breckenridge. It is important to note that the name "Boreas" fails to appear in newspaper and other reports until the early 1880s when the Denver, South Park & Pacific Railroad had launched its service to Breckenridge. That's when the other two passes fell into disuse.

Later, as the gold rush took hold, other crossings of the Snowy Range into the Blue Valley gained prominence. Georgia Pass took prospectors to dazzling Parkville and French Pass put travelers out at Lincoln City, another early gold-rich mine camp.

Evidence for Tarryall, Hamilton and Boreas Passes:
three separate, and different, routes.

Tarryall Pass:
1. The August 20, 1897 edition of the *Rocky Mountain News* lists Colorado mountain passes. It shows Tarryall, Hamilton (early called Breckenridge) and Boreas as three separate pass routes with three different altitudes. These altitudes appear on today's topographic maps as Tarryall, 12,029 feet; Hamilton, 11,680 feet; and Boreas, 11,488 feet.
2. "Over the Mountains," a *Rocky Mountain News* article published April 7, 1880 discusses a railroad route from Como in South Park to Breckenridge. "This route will be admirably adapted for a railroad grade from Como, and the opinion is expressed that if the 59 pass, about two miles west of Breckenridge

pass is selected, that the grade will be about 11,000 feet by cutting a tunnel through a sharp, abrupt range." Tarryall Pass is located on a sharp, abrupt section on Hoosier Ridge. Boreas, ultimately used for the railroad route, is located on a wide saddle with a mild ascent to its summit. (Author's note: "west" in the quote above should be "southwest.")

3. The 1889 book, *Over The Range to the Golden Gate* by Stanley Wood, lists the altitude of Tarryall Pass as 12,176 feet. This differs significantly from Boreas' lower altitude of 11,488 feet. Early travelers, including Colonel John C. Fremont, measured altitude by boiling water, not totally accurate but usually close. Wood's altitude figure for Tarryall Pass is slightly off; the actual figure for the gold rush pass is 12,029 feet.

4. Samuel Bowles in *Colorado, Its Parks and Mountains*, crosses the range at what he calls Breckenridge Pass (really Tarryall) and identifies its altitude as 12,000 feet, consistent with Tarryall Pass but 500-plus feet higher than Boreas Pass.

5. The gold seekers did not include many surveyors and civil engineers. Instead, they scoped out the quickest route, like Tarryall Pass. In contrast, the later railway surveyors and engineers sought the easiest route, a moderate grade necessary for the trains to negotiate, such as Boreas Pass. Early traveler John Young in his *John D. Young and the Colorado Gold Rush*, described in vivid detail the steep summit ascent to Tarryall Pass. Boreas, on the other hand, features a summit ascent with a mild altitude gain.

6. Another source highlighted the final, short, steep ascent to the pass. A reporter for the October 25, 1860 *Western Mountaineer* defined the crossing between what Americans then called Kansas Territory (east of the divide) and Utah Territory (west of the divide):

> *... For seven or eight miles the road was a gentle, steady ascent; and then, after riding up a short, abrupt hill, I was upon the backbone of the American Continent—the dividing ridge between Kansas and Utah. The waters of the Platte and those of the Colorado—emptying respectively into the Atlantic and Pacific— each gush out within pistol shot of the summit. The road passes through a gap, or depression in the range, with sharp, bare mountains rising two thousand feet above it, on either side. It is perfectly practicable and easy for wagons.*

Hamilton Pass:
1. The November 8, 1861-established Breckenridge, Buckskin Joe and Hamilton Wagon Road Company had a branch which followed the left hand fork of Tarryall Creek to the summit of the mountain. The left hand fork of the main or north Tarryall Creek leads to the Hoosier Ridge crossing identified as Hamilton Pass. In contrast, the right fork of Tarryall Creek leads toward Boreas Pass.
2. The Bradford and Blue River toll road, established later on October 11, 1881 went "up the bank of Tarryall Creek following the left hand fork." Again, the left hand fork goes to Hamilton Pass; the right hand fork goes toward Boreas Pass.
3. Bureau of Land Management surveyor George A. Hill's August 5, 1868 map T8S R77W and its 1880s continuation on map T7S R77W show "The Breckenridge Road" as clearly distinct from the later railroad route that crossed the Divide at Boreas Pass. The Breckenridge Road roughly parallels the rail route but stays well to its south, following the left hand fork of Tarryall Creek toward the summit, then descends along Indiana Creek through Indiana Gulch to the Blue River.
4. USGS geologist Charles W. Henderson in his *Mining in Colorado, Professional Paper 138* published in 1926 by the Government Printing Office, Washington, D.C. refers to early-day geologist Raymond who described the Warriors Mark Mine as located "northwest" of the Breckenridge (Hamilton) Pass." That mine is indeed situated northwest of Hamilton Pass but it is located southwest of Boreas Pass.
5. A primitive gold rush map by early cartographer Ebert shows a landmark along Hoosier Ridge called Gilpin's Pillars, which sideline the old wagon road. These landmarks correspond to the two peaks which sideline the old Hamilton Pass saddle at the top of Pennsylvania and Indiana Gulches.
6. *Blasted Beloved Breckenridge* by Mark Fiester used early printed sources to clearly identify the old wagon road as coming through Indiana Gulch, passing old Dyersville and old Conger's Camp, both of which lay well below the rail route. The railroad stayed high on the north side of Indiana Gulch but the wagon road ran northwest from Hamilton Pass, then down the middle of the gulch.

Boreas Pass:
When railroad engineers chose a route for the coming Denver, South

Park & Pacific narrow gauge railway in 1880-81, they chose the present-day Boreas for its comparatively-mild grade. Though still a challenge to mountain railroading, the Boreas route featured a broad, meadowed summit perfect for a new depot and station settlement. This saddle, called Boreas since 1882, had gradually assumed the name Breckenridge Pass. That name, used in the early 1860s for Hamilton Pass, was transferred to Boreas around 1861 as Boreas increased in use for wagon travel. (Boreas is a scenic roadway today.)

Etching from Harpers Illustrated Weekly

These new discoveries—*when* the first prospectors actually arrived and *where* the first prospectors crossed the Snowy Range—lead to another question. *Why* did these early gold-seekers end up on the remote and isolated Blue River?

2

Why Breckenridge?

hy did the Blue River district, blockaded by the Continental Divide, end up as a gold rush destination? Disappointment played a key role. Indian threat pressured gold-seekers. Dazzling gold discoveries in South Park lured prospectors.

The early history of South Park provides the matchstick that ignited on the Blue River. The history of these high country neighbors is forever linked.

In spring 1859 disgruntled Denver prospectors, disappointed in the Auraria Diggings, finally made a big strike at today's Black Hawk. John H. Gregory's bonanza there became known as the Gregory Diggings. A small multitude of hopeful miners rushed to it and many found rich placer claims. Gold seekers, propelled by rumor and mob psychology, have in every North American gold rush abandoned good ground to stampede elsewhere. When a buzz about gold discoveries in South Park, near the head of the South Platte, circulated through the rich Gregory Diggings, men making good wages grabbed their tools, rolled up their bedding, strapped fry pans onto their packs and rushed to what sprang up later as the towns of Tarryall and Hamilton.

1858-59 travelers relied on primitive maps

Virginia McConnell's 1966 book *Bayou Salado* tells how and why both Indian atrocities (perhaps Cheyenne or Arapahoe) and gold fever lured prospectors to Tarryall and beyond the range to the Blue River:

In June of 1859 a group of prospectors . . . came over the mountains from the Gregory Diggings to South Park. Here the group was attacked by Indians but escaped with all scalps intact. On July 9 the party again was set upon and this time Kennedy, Shank and five or six others were killed at what is called Deadman's Gulch, near Kenosha pass.

When word of the murders reached Gregory Diggings, a party set out to catch the guilty Indians. Not finding the culprits, the posse risked stopping to prospect for a while and another group joined them . . .

Among these adventurers were Earl Hamilton, who a year later in 1860 founded the town of Hamilton, and William J. Holman, the founder of Tarryall also in 1860.

The men went up Tarryall Creek north of the present town of Como and found there the old log cabins of John Albert and other trappers. Thinking that prospects looked good there, they lingered and found exciting panning. This strike on the Tarryall, which brought hundreds of prospectors thronging into the area in two weeks, was made about four miles above Como, near the forks of Tarryall Creek and Deadwood Gulch . . .

As the crowd of prospectors arrived, some of them explored the surrounding land. But by August (1859) all of the Tarryall Diggings was staked out, and the claim owners were refusing to subdivide their locations with disappointed late comers.

Traveler-author Samuel Bowles reported 1,000 early arrivals at the Tarryall settlement alone. By 1860, the population of South Park had catapulted to 11,603 according to the U.S. Census.

Among those who left pay dirt at Gregory's Diggings behind was J. Castro, who ended up in Blue River and later became a prominent Coloradan. He sent an account of his trip to the *Rocky Mountain News* which appeared September 17, 1859:

I left Mountain City, Gregory's Diggings, about the 10th Aug., in the company of C. G. Russell, John Hughes, J. H. Gest and others— twelve in number. We crossed the Snowy Range at the head of Chicago Creek, and in three days from home found ourselves in the South Park. We traveled through South Park for two or three days, finding gold everywhere. Messrs. Gest, Sr., Matthews and myself left the main company in search of the new diggings on the head waters of the South Platte, known to the discoverers and claimants by the name of 'Tarry All Diggings," and since known by the thousands who rushed thither as the "Grab All Diggings."... After resting a few days at this point I started over the divide... in company of S. Shoup, R. H. Hyatt, and others, determined to prospect the Middle Park, and the Blue and Grand rivers. After passing over the divide we arrived at the Spaulding Diggings, discovered by Mr. Spaulding and party...

Like Castro and others in high country gold fields, Denver hopefuls heard news of South Park gold.

1858 Denver

Denver Deserted

Not only miners from Gregory Diggings but also disappointed gold seekers from Denver rushed to South Park.

"Everyone in Denver has the blues," Villard commiserated. Happily, the blues evaporated like pipe-tobacco smoke when Denver heard the news of gold in the mountains. A March 5, 1859 letter from John Pouder of Auraria, Kansas Territory (today's Denver) reported that even men building a new town abandoned their project for the Tarryall rush:

There is a company going to start for the "Parks" in a few days. I think there is something rich in them, for some men started a new town above Russelville, and got out logs to build; in the meantime part of them went through to the "Parks" and they came back, sold out, and all hands packed up and left for there again. It is reasonable that they found something that must pay very well, for they left a place which paid a man well—some $3 to $10 per day with pan and rocker.

Oliver Case's letter from Denver City, published April 19, 1859, captures the excitement:

Some of the boys from our train went into the mountains a few days since prospecting, yesterday they came in after provisions and they say that they can make from eight to fifteen dollars a day in the South Park. I shall start on Monday.

They emptied the Auraria diggings in spring, 1859 and poured from the plains to Colorado City (today's Colorado Springs) and up through Manitou to South Park. (Explorers had not yet discovered the shorter routes.) When the impetuous crew arrived and found all of Tarryall's claims staked, they blew up. Ten days of arduous travel over uncharted country left them disappointed, frustrated and angry. Tarryall earned that derisive new name, "Grab-all." Some of the disgruntled returned to Denver. Others looked up, scanned the Snowy Range peaks that barricade South Park from the Blue River and asked themselves, "What lies beyond?" Seeing Tarryall's high quality gold whetted their appetites for more. "Is there gold like that beyond the Snowy Range?"

Disappointment created the catalyst that pushed hardy souls over the fortress rock wall barricading Tarryall from unknown territory beyond.

Ignoring deep spring snows which caused walkers to struggle and wagons to sink, dozens pressed on toward the Divide. They conquered steep grades that caused strong young men to walk only fifteen feet or so before needing to rest. They labored over the staggering ridge that separates South Park and today's Summit County. The reason they endured the struggle: they had heard of gold discoveries on the Blue River.

Among the very first to hazard the climb, Daniel Conner described his Tarryall Pass crossing on May 22, 1859:

After the usual trials and hardships attendant on sleepless nights and constant care, the result mostly of standing guard every alternate night for a period of twelve hours, we arrived at the foot of the cordillera or Snowy Range. We arrived here about the last of May. The mountains presented the most terrible bleak aspect . . .

The next morning the men began their ascent. They had to cut a roadway in the deep snowpack.

We soon came to where the snow was too deep to proceed without tedious difficulties. On the ridges the snow was comparatively solid, with a stout crust on top, but in the innumerable ravines where the snow was drifted the crust would break and let us down. Across those places we began to cut grades with long-handled shovels, of which we were supplied to the extent of one to the man. Thus we cut a railroad grade in appearance, wherever it was absolutely necessary. Continuously at work all day long, as we ascended the Snowy Range until within half-mile of the summit, we were compelled to cut a grade of three hundred paces in length. It became so deep that we couldn't throw the snow out, consequently had to carry it out at each end.

The snow collapsed, plunging Conner into a concealed creek.

We wanted to reach the summit by dark and camp there. It being nearly night enhanced our efforts, and while a number of us were digging away in the lowest place about midway in the grade, the bottom gave away and precipitated us into a wide hidden creek up to our waists in the water. We crawled out, however, and brought the wagon and cattle . . . But every now and then a wheel would break in as deep as the hub, but no farther. We also would break in occasionally, but not deeper than the hips. We arrived on the summit just after dark and pitched camp, after one of the most continuously laborious day's work of taking a wagon and team over the greatest obstacles that I ever know or heard of one passing, before or since.

The remainder of Conner's journey led downhill, a happy relief despite the continued deep snow. The party arrived at the end of the second day of their struggle to cross Tarryall Pass.

The early goldseekers' struggle had a reward: gold as rich as Tarryall's but even more lustrous. Villard saw it in 1859 and wrote, "The appearance of Tarryall gold is unusually clear and bright. It consists of scales and nuggets. The quality of the gold found in the Blue River matches that of the Tarryall gold." More than that, Villard noted, Western Slope gold proved to be more valuable than eastern due to less natural alloy existing in the western.

U. S. Financial Woes Impelled Gold Rushers

Undaunted men exerted mountain-scaling energy like Conner's because the great financial panic of 1857 had devoured fortunes and impoverished many. Conditions rivaled 1932 Depression America. The mostly-young men who entered the 1859 Pikes Peak gold rush faced bleak futures at home. Misery prevailed. When news of gold spread, their hopes soared, enabling them to emigrate to the unknown and uncharted West with little time wasted on pondering the decision.

A *New York Tribune* January 29, 1859 article detailed the woes men left behind:

Ho for Pikes Peak! There is soon to be an immense migration . . . to the new Eldorado. The extensive failure of crops in 1858, the universal pressure of debt, the low prices realized for the fruits of men's labors, the deadness of enterprise, the absence of thrift, render such a migration inevitable.

Gold discoveries in June 1858 by the Georgia Company led by Green Russell leaked out. Stories of $2,000, $3,000 and $6,000 earnings grossly exaggerated the worth of these strikes. Nevertheless, they incited a rush of 100,000 to the new Pikes Peak gold fields.

A colorful tide of the masses moved across the Great Plains. A March, 1859 letter written in Atchison, Kansas described the improbable parade:

> *Hundreds of persons en route for the gold regions, traveling in every conceivable manner . . . some with mules, others with handcarts, and one company brought up the rear with the running-gear of a buggy, upon which was loaded mining tools, camp fixtures, etc. and was drawn by eleven men, the foremost of which was a young man of delicate appearance, dressed in a fine cloth coat, stovepipe hat, and patent leather boots.*

When these impractically-garbed travelers arrived in Denver, gold rush promoter Horace Greeley declared, even their mothers would fail to recognize them. He witnessed the exhausted boys "straggling into this place, hideously hirsute, recklessly ragged, barefoot and brown, dust-covered and with eyes shielded by goggles from the glare of the prairie sun."

No matter how jubilant they began, many gold seekers who ventured from the Midwest boundaries of the United States to cross the vast untamed prairies got as far as today's Denver, then in Kansas Territory, and found scanty gold at the much-touted diggings. Sputtering the 1850s putdown of "Humbug!" they beat a retreat from the western territories back to the States. The rush back swelled to tidal wave proportions. *Harper's Weekly,* the popular 1850s magazine, told the story on August 13, 1859, just about the time Ruben J. Spaulding struck gold on the Blue River:

> *An estimated 100,000 gold seekers set out for Colorado in the spring of 1859, many of them lured by the guidebooks, most of them romantic fortune seekers. Of the 50,000 who actually reached the gold fields, probably half or more quickly became discouraged at the hard work and small returns and started home. This June report of traffic on the Platte River road tells of meeting 5,000 of these "Go Backs" in only ten days. Many others pressed on to California. In Denver, some of these deluded men, infuriated by the deception practiced upon them, had inflicted reprisals and threatened to burn the town. Two guidebook authors in Denver were abused and threatened with lynching . . .*

3

Picture the Prospectors

I ronically, just as Front Range gold rushers turned back, prospectors on the isolated Blue struck gold. The "go-backs" missed the find that later boosted the Blue River to Colorado Territory's leading placer producer. As the disappointed gold seekers departed, Spaulding's group labored to reroute the river channel to expose gold deposits, to build sluice boxes which retrieved the gold and to create ditches to carry the water so crucial to placer mining success.

Placer mining retrieves free gold—glacier-eroded gold scraped from original deposits—from existing waterways or from deposits on banks and benches laid down by ancient waterways now gone. It uses water to wash the gold from accompanying sand, gravels and dirt. Hardrock or lode mining extracts gold from veins embedded in rock.

Three mining districts soon divided the Blue River Diggings: Pollack District at the south end of today's Breckenridge, Independent District in the middle and Spaulding District at the north end. The Spaulding District, fairly typical of the others, measured three miles in length, extending 1½ miles north of the discovery hole and 1½ miles south of it. The miners identified their location as "the Blue Fork of the Colorado River, Utah Territory." Each claim occupied 100 feet of riverbank, except the discovery claim which had 200 feet. The miners immediately organized a plan to turn the Blue River to expose bedrock and the gold that would have, over eons, collected there. Each man who labored at this for the required 10 hours per day received $3, good wages in 1859. Those who elected not to work paid into an expense fund for the dam and ditch.

Ruben J. Spaulding remembered the hard work: " . . . I made three toms *(a long tom is an extended version of the miner's sluice box, about*

Tent City

20 feet long) and went to mining in water ankle deep, and having nothing better to wear on my feet, I roped them with pieces of a saddle blanket. The first day's work netted me $10 and a bad cold." *($10 was a sum to cause jubilation in recession-ridden 1859.)*

Felix Poznansky numbered among those who arrived at the Blue River Diggings well before Spaulding's party. He too set about ditching. His hand-written "Early History of Mining on the Blue River and Vicinity" records in pencil the mining districts formed as the 1859 summer progressed: (His spelling and grammar are preserved.)

> *Sometime in July 59 I came on the Blue. Doctor Boyd a few days before came over across the range and helped to organize the Independent District and took a claim for me No. 40. There were then 3 districts organized on the Blue, namely the Polack, the Independent and Spalding. All the work going on when I landed was the Iloff Brothers had a water wheel pump going in the Spalding District. Very little work don in Polack Districkt. We in the Independent District survaid a ditch to turn the water out of the channel. As the Californians mentioned that all the gold was to be found on Bed Rock of the stream. Those of the miners that were not let astray by those smart ones went to work on the Bars don well that summer. We on the other hand fooled away all summer trying to make the ditch hold the water when it would not hold one-fourth of the water that came poring down the Blue. So we had the same truble of enlarging. There was very little gold taken out of the Blue that year.*

Poznansky's memory brings focus to our blurred snapshot of summer, 1859 along the Blue. Additional clarity comes from a recently-uncovered 1859 record.

Researcher Retrieves Spaulding Log Book

Due to the efforts of historian Bill Fountain, a transcript of the original and long-missing Spaulding Diggings Log Book is available for historical research. Fountain's transcript sharpens the fading image of 150 years ago and reveals just how the miners conducted the business of their district. The initial meeting of the Spaulding Diggings miners took place on August 15, 1859, five days after gold discovery. The prime movers in that meeting were J. S. Keatts, who became president; John G. Randall, Secretary pro tem; a man named Coonley; George E. Dyer; Colonel Samuel G. Jones; and Asher Stevens.

The book records the initial claims of many more miners, proof that more prospectors than the Spaulding party's original 14 occupied the Blue River Valley in summer, 1859. The names of the claimants who filed on August 15, for the record, are:

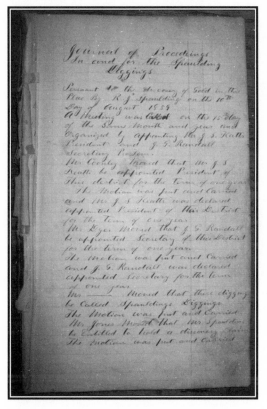

Claims North of Discovery
E. N. Tuttle
Samuel G. Jones
George E. Dyer
W. N. Shaw
William Rolen
Gustavus A. Williams
H. Eby
James Vandusen
J. M. Piper
Albert Yerhime

Claims South of Discovery
John G. Randall
Ruben J. Spaulding
   (Discovery)
Asher M. Stevens
J. W. Mitchell
William H. Iliff
Jonah Fink
John Rolen
J. S. Keatts
Thomas Fleming
Lewis Prell
N. Henry
Lysander Pollard
R. R. Bartle

Fragile parchment pages, elegant script writing, grace old Spaulding Log Book.

In addition, claims filed the next day, August 16, included Edward McDavitt, Justus A. Megargel, Fred K. Kershaw, Oscar F. Eddy, Evan Davis and Daniel Woodman. Though more miners recorded claims later, the total in just the first two days is 29 men. Some of these men surely stampeded from neighboring Blue River placers to claim near the new Spaulding strike.

With a mining district now organized, placer work shifted into high gear. The mining district turned former rivals into a team. Experienced miners shared their knowledge with those who possessed large hopes but little mining skill. Many were raw beginners who missed golden opportunities and wasted precious discovery time. The Spaulding party together took on the ambitious task of turning the then-raging Blue River—a project hampered by leaky channel walls and the riverbed's ample layer of glacier-deposited boulders.

Fort Mary B

A 1,500-strong band of Utes camped five miles down the Blue gave the miners no trouble, according to author John D. Young. However, their presence served as a constant reminder that the new arrivals had claimed a promised land inhabited by potentially cantankerous natives with more than squatters' rights to the gold-laced real estate. The Spaulding District miners devised the idea of building a fort for protection against possible Indian attack. As September leaves turned the nearby slopes to the miners' favorite color, builders heightened the racket of rock moving and gravel shoveling with other sounds. Trees smashed to the ground and axes rang as miners notched the logs to raise Fort Mary B. (The structure bore many names, including Fort Independence, Jones Fort, Fort Mary Bigelow and Fort Meribeh but Fort Mary B is the name the Spaulding miners chose.)

The sod-roofed fort held block dwellings all facing inward in a hollow square. It formed a compound that its residents considered highly defensible. Builders made the two entrances easy to guard and its green-log construction hard to burn. Inside the fort Mr. Idding's store sold miners' goods and clothing. Attack from the mild-mannered Utes never materialized but the fort provided a winter dwelling for 20 or so hardy prospectors, one even-hardier woman and four children, according to prolific correspondent William A. Smith writing to the *Western Mountaineer.*

John Young described the fort in his *John D. Young and the Colorado Gold Rush:*

> *The fort was a very strong looking building being made of large pine logs about ten feet high inclosing about one acre and loopholed on every side for musketry.*

The Utes, called the black-skinned Indians for their swarthy color, traveled as hunter-gatherers. They camped along the Blue enroute to Hoosier Pass and South Park in July following the buffalo herds. The high passes, Georgia, French, Boreas, Tarryall, Hamilton and Hoosier emerged first as buffalo crossings, then native people's routes. The Utes lived lightly on the land, stopping to hunt on Vail Pass, where a 6,800 year-old carbon-dated campsite remained. They gathered roots, berries and bulbs along the Blue. In South Park they hunted buffalo and dug petrified wood which they hardened in fire for projectile points.

Though ferocious to their enemies, especially the Arapahoe and Cheyenne, the Utes generally extended a welcome to white miners. Expert horsemen, the short, stocky Utes remained in their ancient homeland longer than did many other American tribes. They were marched away under guard of U.S. militia in 1879-80, never to return.

The 1,500 Utes probably slipped away to their winter campsite. By October 4, 1859 miner and medical man Dr. E. H. Boyd wrote a letter to the *Rocky Mountain News* from his new home at "Fort Independence on the Blue River."

> *... We have found the bed of the stream very rich (for, mind you, we have dammed the river) and I have no hesitance in crying out 'Eureka.' We are able to pan out from three to eight grains of the precious metal, to the pan on an average, within six inches of the top of the ground. We are all 'OK,' except for one thing, namely, flour and bacon is scarce, and we dislike to go after it. Many of us expect to winter here if we can get provisions. There is plenty of game, such as black bear, elk, moose, deer, black and grey wolves, rabbits, beaver, and better than all, the finest fish I ever saw, and 'I haven't always been at home.' Will not some of your provision merchants send out some hundred sacks of flour? There is no difficulty in reaching here, the road is good and plain. My opinion is that four wagon-loads of provisions could be sold here in one day, and that at figures which would pay.*
>
> *We have seen no Indians, and the old mountain boys say they seldom come this way. We are having quite a good time at present, and the health of the miners is excellent.*
>
> *Yours truly,*
> *E. H. Boyd, M.D.*

The Fort, located just north of what later became Breckenridge, sat on an "island" of land between the Blue River and the placer mining channel dug by the Spaulding District miners. Historians have long known its general location. However, in 2008 avid field researchers Rick Skovlin, Rick Hague, Maureen Nicholls and Bill Fountain pinpointed a

Fixin' flapjacks

site on the south-facing wing of the City Market shopping center as their choice of the Fort Mary B site. Early sources indicated that the fort lay northwest of the old Jones Mill/Breckenridge Smelter. Nicholls' photo of the mill, with the Ten Mile peaks in the background, helped identify the fort site. No clues existed because a 1900s gold dredge obliterated both the smelter and Fort Mary B remains.

The story behind Fort Mary B's name is like the Fort itself—an enigma. We know from the Spaulding log book that the name honors the first white woman to cross the range. A June 1998 Summit Historical Society newsletter suggested that Mary B. Bunker, born in Indiana in 1840, crossed the range in 1859. John L. Dyer performed her marriage to Clement Bunker on November 7, 1862 in Park County. When she died in 1911 her obituary called her "the first white woman to cross the Breckenridge Range."

But wait. Another female contender for the namesake, dug up by the late Summit Historical Society researcher Naomi Fleming, vies for naming honors. The elusive story focuses on a Mrs. James P. Marksbury who wintered on the Blue River that first 1859 season. James Marksbury came to Blue River earlier that year, located a claim at what soon became bustling Delaware City (today's Breckenridge Golf Course land) and built a log cabin. His wife, a toddler and a newborn joined him. The infant, Jeanette, became the first white baby to live in what became Summit County.

Thirty-five years later, Ruben J. Spaulding remembered the name of the first white woman in Summit County as Mrs. Maybery. No matter what the spelling, two facts support the possibility that the Spaulding miners named the fort for Mrs. Marksbury. First, this woman arrived on the scene in 1859 with two children. Second, she spent the winter of 1859 here. No other white woman did.

Her baby girl Jeanette (Nettie) grew up in Breckenridge and married a miner, William F. Eberlein. Their Breckenridge home, built in 1877 ranks as one of the town's earliest surviving residences. The Eberlein home, moved from Main Street, now resides in the Milne Park on Harris Street.

Jeanette's own baby daughter, who died the day of her birth, April 6, 1879, was buried in Breckenridge's first primitive cemetery at the town's south end. The tiny grave remained there for over a century, then, with a great community turnout, moved to Valley Brook Cemetery.

Jeanette's younger brother, was the first white child born in Summit County. Aptly named Summit Marksbury, he loved to run. And run he did, often cruising over Hoosier Pass and back. He won a prestigious European race in London.

Was Fort Mary B named after his trail-blazing mother? The answer remains obscure. One thing is more certain. Mrs. Marksbury ranks as Summit County's first woman pioneer.

Not every miner chose to remain at the fort. John Randall, Spaulding Diggings secretary-recorder, wintered in New Mexico. Like many 59ers, the 27-year old Randall was a man of integrity, hard work and honor. A natural leader, he won election to Minnesota's first state legislature in 1857. He prospected the Blue in the early 1860s. After Civil War service as a government recruiting officer, he became a member of Colorado's Territorial legislature in 1870 and 72. His death in 1897 brought a flood of praise for a man with a "noble heart."

A second miner to miss winter 1859 at the fort was Felix Poznansky. Entrusted by the miners to bring in vital food supplies for fort residents, he had struggled to reach Denver to purchase the supplies. Snow stopped the wagon shipment at Tarryall and blocked Poznansky's return. Supplies trickled in by foot.

PIONEER PROFILE: Felix Poznansky

A man of bright intellect, creativity and adventurous spirit, Felix Poznansky left his stamp on early Breckenridge. He played a key role as a catalyst in the town's foundation and continued to revisit Breckenridge over the following four decades. Endued with a vibrant sense of history, he recorded early events in his mining history essay, authored newspaper articles and gave interviews. These contributions add valuable texture to the hard-to-capture fabric of 1859-60 Breckenridge life.

Determined to make his way to the United States, Poznansky left his native Poland and walked to Paris. He then stowed away on a ship bound for America. The Polish immigrant headed west. On the way, he managed to acquire an ox team and drove the animals across the plains. The travelers used oxen for hauling wagons and eventually butchered them for much-needed meat when they reached their destination. He reached Denver on June 16, 1859, a true Colorado 59er.

According to an August 25, 1900 *Summit County Journal* article, Poznansky soon joined a party of five gold seekers headed for the rich diggings in Gregory Gulch. Like so many others, Poznansky's party ignited to the wildfire news of "pound diggings" (one pound of gold per man per day) in what reports called "the New Eldorado" in South Park. Though the gold enthusiasts lacked any sure knowledge of the bonanza's exact location, they outfitted in Denver and followed the gold rush route to today's Colorado Springs, then into South Park. New information from prospectors in the Park directed them to Tarryall.

There Poznansky met a man from Blue River who boasted of that area's rich placer bars. The adventurous Pole packed flour, hard tack, tea and blankets on his back, mounted Tarryall Pass and arrived in Blue River Diggings to camp at the present South Main Street-Park Avenue intersection in today's Breckenridge.

When tapped to make the Denver supplies trip that fall, Poznansky baked up all his flour in three fry-pan batches of bread, took an inch slab of bacon, a little tea and set out for Denver. He crossed snow-covered high passes on this meager diet! The miners faced some pressure to get winter provender because they had received a September surprise. Poznansky remembered in his April

Felix Poznansky

24, 1906 *Breckenridge Bulletin* article, "we awoke on a September morning to find about two feet of snow."

The enterprising Poznansky managed, after weeks of failed effort, to persuade Denver merchants Ming and Solomon to bring a load of food and supplies to Blue River. The goods got as far as Tarryall, hampered by heavy snows. Blue River residents hired a Norwegian to haul supplies by foot over the Divide at ten cents per pound. This, Poznansky said, "made Blue River an expensive residence." Flour ran as high as $15-$20 a sack (a week's wages) on the 1858-59 frontier, coffee a hefty 50 cents per pound and whiskey $8 a barrel.

His tough assignment to obtain winter supplies complete, Poznansky focused on gaining the townsite claim for the new town
of Independence. When he lost that advantage to George Spencer,
it aggravated his personal woes. As a raw beginner at mining, he
invested precious capital in an *arrastre* to pulverize ore, so ill-de-
signed and poorly-built that it tumbled down a hillside to its ruin.
(Author's note: An *arrastre* is a Spanish ore milling device. The
circular trough holds the ore, while heavy stones dragged by a
horse or mule grind the ore.)

However, sweet consolation lay in store for the disappointed
Pole. He enjoyed the good fortune in 1860 to venture with three
other prospectors south on the Blue to Quandary Peak near
Hoosier Pass. Poznansky and a companion, who separated from
the party, struck rich silver at a mine they named the Pulaski "after
a country man of mine who fought in the American revolution."
The pair formed a mining district and the literate Poznansky
ended up as secretary-recorder. Because his comrade could neither read nor write, the man was promoted to president. The partners, hungry and impoverished, got a bonanza—but not from the
silver, though it had high value. Instead they "mined the miners,"
by selling them food at the exorbitant going rates. This way they
pioneered a lucrative mercantile activity that flourished once
Breckenridge began. Poznansky recalled,

> As soon as we got home the news spread like wild fire that I
> was recorder of some valuable Leads. (Author's note: a lead is
> a mineral-bearing vein deposited between two walls, usually
> of granite.) And the Dollars (which was the fee for recording)
> came in faster than we possiby could get (gold) out of the Blue.
> In a few days we had two sacks of flour. A German above us
> killed an ox we bought 3 quarters of him and salted it down.
> We also bought from him 60 lbs of tallow which came in handy
> to fry dounuts in besides other things. Was not this a Godsend?

Divine blessing didn't stop there. The lucky prospectors
gloated. They experienced the good luck of buying the food in the
same place they sold it. Thus they avoided the expense and labor
of hauling over the Divide. But the best was yet to come:

> So you see it saved us a gread ill of hardship, besides the above
> bill of fare we had for a change jack rabids whenever we
> wanted and as many as we wanted just the same as you would

When winter unleashed its alpine fury, the miners were tucked safely into the log confines of their fort. Supplies furnished their biggest challenge. Although abundant game staved off hunger, their cravings for coffee, tea, bacon, tobacco, flour, soap and other comforts went unsatisfied once snow blocked supplies. Boredom created the second biggest challenge. Imagine the confinement of winter days in an isolated and uninhabited mountain valley without newspapers, magazines, books, television, computers, games, restaurants, social events or any access to the outside world.

It's no wonder that the Spaulding party's two Norwegians, Balce and Christian Weaver, recently from Henry County, Illinois, set about making wooden skis. By February, they traversed the neighboring countryside on those heavy 12-foot spruce boards. Six miles down the Blue in Gold Run Gulch their lightning cry of "Gold" split the cloud of boredom. Probably using fires to melt the snow and the frozen earth, the Weaver boys discovered stunning riches in placer gold beneath eight feet of February snow. Gold Run became a name synonymous with Midas riches and produced dazzling yields over decades to come. Balce and Christian Weaver took home a reputed 96 pounds of gold their first season. Gold Run's output became a significant contributor to Summit County's 1859-1867 production of placer gold. The amount estimated by geologist C. W. Henderson: a then-incredible $5,150,000.

Which proved more significant—the amazing gold strike? Or Colorado's first recorded ski event? The Weaver boys launched a snow sport that years later made Colorado famous and established Breckenridge as a world-class resort destination.

4

Envision the New Town

Prospectors holed up at Fort Mary B for the 1859-60 winter battled boredom. So did miners camped at Tarryall, 16 miles east across the Snowy Range. One of many who winter-camped in tents there, George E. Spencer, had nothing much to do but think. He developed a plan to snag townsite rights for a new community at the Blue River Diggings. A second contender, Felix Poznansky, hatched a similar plan. Since the two chose separate locations—Spencer's near Spaulding's strike and Poznansky at the Independent Mining District (today's Breckenridge town core)—there first appeared little cause for contention. The two even conferred over their parallel plans at the Tarryall camp.

Poznansky recalled in a May 12, 1906-published letter to the *Breckenridge Bulletin:*

> *One night at the camp fire a man by the name of Geo. Spencer exhibited a map of a town named Breckenridge. It looked fine on paper and I asked where that town was located. He told me that he had been sent out by Denver capitalists to lay out a town on the Blue. I asked him where and he said at the Fort. I joked with him by telling him I was going to have an opposition town a mile above him.*

Spencer attracted powerful partners. As early as December 28, 1859, The Golden-based *Western Mountaineer* published a new-town article naming the men involved—an impressive alliance:

> *BRECKENRIDGE—This is the name of a new town which has been laid out and platted, situated in the Middle Park, upon the Blue River. We have been shown a map of the town in connection with the surrounding country, by Col. S. G. Jones; and from his description we judge it to be a fine point for a mining town. It has the advantage of an abundance of excellent building timber and rich gold diggings within its borders. We understand a steam saw-mill will be located there at an early day . . . The officers of the company are as follows: President, Gen. R. B. Bradford; Vice President, S. G. Jones; Treasurer, L. W. Bliss; Secretary, G. E. Spencer, who are ex officio directors, together with Messrs. C. P. Hall, E. James and B. D. Williams. From the*

*well-known energy and enterprise of these gentlemen, we have no
doubt a flourishing town will be built up.*

These men had already distinguished themselves in Colorado.
Colonel Samuel G. Jones, a summer-1859 pioneer and California gold
rush veteran, filed a claim in the Spaulding District on August 15, 1859.
He demonstrated leadership in drafting laws for that first mining district. He later chaired the Bloomfield Town Company board in 1860
when miners struck silver near Quandary Peak. He wrote informative
letters to the *Rocky Mountain News* describing mining progress on the
Blue. A civil engineer who surveyed the Breckenridge townsite, his reputation grew in Denver and throughout the territory. The many-named
Fort Mary B also bore his name, Jones Fort, in its earliest days.

General Robert B. Bradford, the group's president, built the first
wagon toll road which made transport of vital supplies to the Blue River
Diggings possible. B. D. Williams was the Washington politico and Con-
gressional lobbyist who later served as agent to secure a postoffice for
a fledgling Breckenridge.

With this kind of alliance, Spencer could not fail to secure the new
townsite. However, when he tramped over the range to check his chosen
site, Spencer found that an interloper had already claimed the desig-
nated land near Fort Mary B for use as a ranch. He probably entertained
the less-than-noble notion of commandeering Poznansky's site. And he
did just that.

The conflict moved into high gear when the contenders had a chance
meeting near the top of the Continental Divide. Poznansky, who had
gotten a wagon load of supplies from Denver as far as Ming's store in
Tarryall, was doing a winter tramp from Blue River to Tarryall. Spencer
had camped for the night near the summit, on his way to Blue River
and the townsite grab.

When Poznansky heard of Spencer's duplicity, he hashed over the
problem with Tarryall friend, supply freighter and storekeeper, John
Ming. The pair formed a partnership with William A. Smith and others,
including a knowledgeable man named Lee. Lee informed them that
federal law conferred the 320-acre townsite ownership rights upon the
entrepreneur who built the "first improvement," a structure which had
to be at least eight logs high. The man who owned the townsite could
then sell lots, a lucrative development venture.

Years later, in an August 25, 1900 *Summit County Journal* interview,
Poznansky remembered how his son, Wolfe, and his friend, Smith, came
to his aid:

*I was on my way to Tarryall where all our belongings were stored,
and in about four miles from that place I heard my name called from*

a tent. It was the man Spencer who called. He charged me with hav-
ing jumped his townsite. I asked him if he had not told me his town-
site was at the Fort. He said he had changed his mind. I told him he
could not have our townsite. He said he would get it, and when I
asked how, he said, "by first improvement."

Here was a fine situation. He was four miles on his way to the town-
site and I was going the other way. As soon as I got to Tarryall I went
to Ming's store and told him the situation. We decided that it was
necessary to start a letter that very night to my boy instructing him
to start a house at once. A man volunteered to go, and who should it
be but my friend, Mr. Smith. About eleven o'clock he got started,
with his snow shoes on. He got to the Blue about daylight and by ten
o'clock, when Spencer arrived, our house was eight logs high, and
laid on six feet of snow. When Spencer saw the boys at work he called
out, "stop, boys, I'm done."

This surprise caught the cool-headed Spencer off guard. When he collected his considerable wits, the would-be developer realized he was neither done, nor undone. Intelligent but less educated, Poznansky presented no match for Spencer.

Spencer was the son of aristocrats and educated as an attorney. Because he knew the law and possessed a strong bent for politics, he outsmarted Poznansky at every turn. With no hesitation, Spencer used his wily ways to seize the advantage. He recovered from his initial shock when he too arrived the day of the Poznansky cabin-raising. Devising a plan, he persuaded the Independent District miners to let him survey the land, another key step in the townsite application, promising each one of twelve choice lots. He protested that he would take only the left-over land for himself. The men agreed. Poznansky, seeing his loss of support, bowed out.

Years later, after a distinguished Spencer had served both in the Civil War and as U.S. Senator from Alabama, Poznansky referred to the then-Southerner with the slur of "carpet-bagger."

PIONEER PROFILE: General George E. Spencer

Despite his tarnished reputation with Felix Poznansky, General George Eliphas Spencer proved himself a distinguished and prominent American. During the Civil War, according to the Alabama Department of Archives and History, he commanded a Civil War cavalry brigade in Sherman's famous march to the sea. On

July 21, 1868, Spencer was elected Republican Senator in Congress for a six-year term. He won re-election in 1873.

George Eliphas Spencer was born November 1, 1836 in New York State. He was the son of Dr. Gordon P. Spencer, a U.S. Army surgeon in the War of 1812. He descended from the honorable John C. Spencer and Ambrose Spencer, statesmen and lawyers.

Spencer received a liberal education at Montreal College in Canada, and then returned to his hometown, Watertown, New York, to study law. He went to Iowa, where in 1857 he was admitted to the bar, and then chosen secretary of the Iowa State Senate for its 1857-58 session. During 1859-60, he joined the Colorado gold rush, founded the townsite of Breckenridge and secured appointment as the town's first postmaster. Spencer never served in that post. He gave it to storekeeper O. A. Whittemore. With the outbreak of the Civil War in 1861, he returned East to enlist in the U.S. Army and served as chief of staff to the notable Major-General Grenville M. Dodge, who after the war laid out the Union Pacific railroad's route.

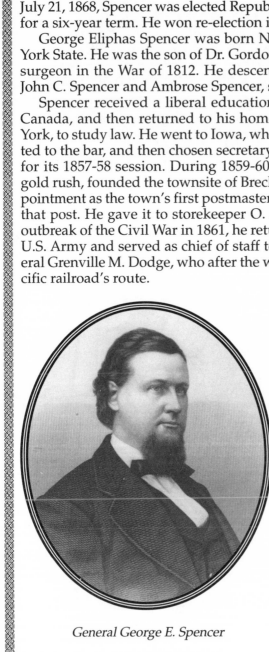

General George E. Spencer

In 1863 Civil War service, Spencer recruited and raised the first regiment of Alabama cavalry, U.S. Army, composed of mountaineers of that state. He was brevetted a brigadier general for gallantry on the field, March 13, 1865. Clearly, the man reviled by Felix Poznansky risked his life to become a Civil War hero.

After the war, he resumed the practice of law in Decatur, Alabama. As a Senator in the 45th Congress, he served as chairman of the prestigious committee on military affairs.

He spent most of his last two years on a ranch in Nevada, where he had mining interests. On February 19, 1893 at age 57, he died while on a visit to Washington, D.C.

Spencer left a sour taste on the tongue of some Breckenridge citizens. A few years later, they took over rights to Spencer's townsite and redistributed rightful ownership by seizure, or "jumping." Vindication came to rival Poznansky when he ended up owning part of the Breckenridge townsite long after the double-dealing episode. He wrote years later:

In the winter of 1863-4 I was wintering in Central City and received a letter from Judge (George) Bissell which read: "Whereas, the Breckenridge townsite never lived up to their agreement made with the Independent Townsite company, we therefore have jumped the townsite and included you in the jumping, and you are entitled to one-twelfth of it."

How Breckenridge Got Its Name

George Spencer's opportunism caused a present-day debate over the naming of Breckenridge. Sources from 1859 clearly state that Spencer's townsite alliance named their new community Breckenridge. Yet the town's first postoffice bore the name Breck*in*ridge. Later the spelling returned to the original, Breck*en*ridge. What's the real story?

Was it named for an explorer or a vice president? Why did the spelling bounce back and forth? As we will see, two men with similar last names played key roles.

Again, researcher Bill Fountain has mined historical archives to unearth informational nuggets that resolve confusion over the town's name. Fountain's version stitches several arguments together. Here is the story:

Breckenridge Pass: This book earlier mentioned Thomas E. Breckenridge. He disappeared west over the Continental Divide from the 1845 Colonel John C. Fremont Colorado expedition in search of a runaway mule. After a two-day absence, Breckenridge returned, pulling the obstinate pack animal behind him. Fremont named the Hoosier Ridge saddle they crossed Breckenridge Pass. When the 1860 prospectors crossed the Snowy Range, they used Breckenridge Pass, calling it by that name. (Later road builders named it Hamilton Pass when they pushed through the 1861 post road. Spencer and partners took that Breckenridge name for their new town.)

Postoffice Problem: Spencer faced a challenge. To succeed, his remote settlement required a postoffice. Washington regarded the nowhere new town, located in Utah Territory, with disdain. (The Front Range lay in the better-known Kansas Territory.) So the opportunist Spencer simply adjusted the spelling of the town name, inserting an "i" where the "e" in Breckenridge had been. Through the intervention of Washington insider B. D. Williams, Spencer informed President Buchanan's prestigious vice president, John Cabell Breckinridge that he had named the new mineral capitol "Breckinridge" after that illustrious gentleman. A flattered vice president pulled the necessary strings and Breckinridge obtained a postoffice as quickly as January 18, 1860. George Spencer pulled another plum out of the pie—the job of postmaster.

A month later, the new town became part of a just-formed Colorado Territory.

Early mail: June 19 letter arrived in Ft. Dodge July 13.

Rebel Denounced: When Civil War broke out, former vice president Breckinridge, now a U.S. senator, enlisted in the Confederate Army. His colleagues promptly pitched him out of Congress. Equally incensed, citizens of the gold camp bearing his name yanked out the "i" to distance themselves from the rebel, plugged the "e" back in—and the case closed.

1860 Boom Detonates

Rumors of dazzling gold strikes continued to filter across the range and ticked like an explosive device until May, 1860 when the bomb blew. As snow melted from the impenetrable Continental Divide, prospectors, pack trains, ox-drawn wagons, mules and horses loaded with pickaxes, gold pans and shovels shot toward the bases of Hoosier, Breckenridge, Tarryall, French and Georgia Passes to exploit the Blue Valley's hidden wealth. In the darkness after midnight when the spring snow hardened into a firm crust, they made their crossing attempts. Some had to abandon work animals and wagons. Some ditched valuable supplies. But they made it. The placer boom began.

Gold seekers from every state and immigrants from many countries poured over the passes at a rate of 100 to 200 per day. From the paltry few who had wintered at Fort Mary B the population catapulted, some sources say as high as 8,000. Fanning out from Breckenridge, they penetrated gulches and valleys. They unearthed gold everywhere. Canadian French Pete discovered French Gulch gold northeast of town. Illinois Gulch to the southeast yielded placer nuggets. Nearby what was then called Nigger Gulch gave up $6,000 in gold during summer, 1860. But the fabled wealth that epitomized the American Dream exploded into frenzy at Parkville, a new town below Georgia Pass. Prospectors made $20 per day per man in Parkville's gold-latticed Georgia and Humbug gulches (when a bushel of tomatoes cost five cents) and took out a total of $3 million in gold that first summer. Gold brought only $16-$18 per ounce then, not the nearly $1,000 per ounce of early 2009. Today's value of that Breckenridge gold would prove staggering.

A log settlement arose to accommodate a rising tide of prospectors.

Breckenridge boomed. Four stores were thrown up to supply miners. "We can now buy anything in the line of provisions or clothing," William A. Smith reported to the *Rocky Mountain News.* Saloons and hotels opened in tents amid the frenzy of prospector influx.

Smith's letter to the *News* May 23, 1860 enthused:

We have three store houses under way, two in Breckenridge, and one in Fort Mary B., which will be stocked with a variety of miners goods soon. Lumber is being sold at twenty dollars per hundred feet. Beef at fourteen and sixteen cents per pound. Emigrants are pouring in at

*the rate of about fifty a day, with occasionally one returning. One fel-
low upon reaching the summit, scribed the following on a tree,
'twenty miles to hell and back.'*

Travel continued to be an exhausting effort for the 1860 gold seekers
who scaled the Continental Divide at precipitous Tarryall Pass. John
Young's journal appears in the book, *John D. Young and the Colorado
Gold Rush,* and details an early-day backpacking jaunt for two city boys
in May, 1860. It is included almost in its entirety because of the vivid
picture it paints, one captured nowhere else. Let's begin with the boys'
approach to the divide:

*Grand, gloomy and frowning the sight was enough to deter a stout
heart from attempting to scale those forbidding and seemingly impassible barriers of ice and snow. We kept boldly on our course and
by night we camped just at the snow line.*

*. . . After the fatigue of walking about six miles up hill with your
knees aching every step you took it was a luxury to get lying down
anywhere especially as the night was cold and chilly . . .*

*I woke up at daylight shivering and benumbed from the cold. I felt
an unusual weight on my body and on pushing the blanket from my
head I perceived that we had a heavy fall of snow during the night.
Things looked wretched in the extreme. Our fire was entirely extin-
guished. The wretched mule stood near by covered with a white
blanket of snow so weak and exhausted by hunger and cold that he
was not able to shake the snow from his back.*

*We prepared some breakfast and by sunrise were once more ascend-
ing towards that far off lofty peak. The trail was entirely obliterated
by the snow that had fallen during the night. We now had to guide
our course by a pocket compass. It now became awful hard to go
ahead. Sometimes we would get into drifts over our armpits. There
was also great danger of walking over some concealed precipice and
being dashed to pieces. The mule showed signs of giving out and I
thought we must have the poor thing to perish on the mountains.
We sat down nearly in despair at the cheerless looking prospect when
we heard some merry voices ahead.*

The party passing by included some friends who took the bedrag-
gled mule back to Tarryall.

*We now had to arrange our packs and make them as convenient as
possible to carry on our shoulders. We had each a pair of blankets
weighting about five pounds each ten pounds of flour three pounds
of meat two pounds of sugar one pound of coffee a coffee pot and*

frying pan making in all about fifteen pounds for each to carry. We strapped the bundles on our shoulders and started bravely up the mountain. The sun now shone out pretty hot melting the snow and making it very disagreeable. The summit now was about a mile off but it did not look one fourth that distance. The incline was becoming more steep so that we had to sit down and rest about every fifteen yards.

Oh it was terrible hard work climbing up there. Sometimes I would fix a point and say we would make that our next resting place. We would start and strain every sinew to reach it but it would be impossible. Ere we got half way we would be panting like a sheep on a hot day. Our knees would get weak and shaky and we would drop down utterly exhausted and lay full length on the snow until we would get revived. The pack small as it was by this time had grown into an enormous burden. We thought if we were rid of it that we could make the journey without much inconvenience and we were almost tempted to throw it away.

Sublime views from the summit heartened the pair who did finally reach Breckenridge.

Travelers enjoyed the benefits of a rough road later in 1860. Soon the 1861-chartered Denver, Bradford and Blue River Toll Road, company-opened and maintained, eased travel and freight hardships. The toll fees, though stiff, failed to equal the physical cost of packing over the pass. Fees were $1 per wagon and team, each additional span 25 cents; horsemen 10 cents; livestock 5 cents; sheep 1 cent. People traveling to church services or a funeral paid no toll.

The May and June early-birds of the 1860 rush found to their dismay that they lost the golden worm. A huge spring run-off which expanded streams into torrents and creeks into raging riptides prevented all thought of placer mining until at least July. (Old-timers say that the Blue River, prior to present water diversion, would rip a bucket from your hand at normal flow.)

Letters Capture 1860 Breckenridge

James Fergus who arrived from Little Falls, Minnesota on July 10, 1860, wrote letters to his wife Pamela. He lamented taking no gold out of the Blue due to the torrent of runoff water. Instead, he used his ample free time to build a 20 x 24 foot house on his mining claim and another in the new town of Breckenridge. The town company promised settlers four free lots when they purchased just one—if they built a good-sized structure. Fergus admitted that his 1½ story Breckenridge building was too large but said he planned to sell it or keep it for a friend to use as a store.

James Fergus

The less industrious never built at all. Fergus described little bowers, shelters made of branches or saplings of spruce or pine, which prospectors occupied for a night or two. When one moved on, another quickly plunked down his pack there.

By July the Fergus letters glowed with word-pictures of wildflower-punctuated green meadows, some even suspended beneath the highest crags. He sallied forth on a prospecting trip where he sighted droves of elk, buffalo, bighorn sheep and bear with their cubs.

Slogging over summit passes carrying bed, board and mining tools on that trip acquainted Fergus with a new understanding of the words "hard work." He rated scaling mountains as more demanding than walking through deep snow. Even more challenging, however, was the daily labor of mining. By July 30 he moaned that standing 12 hours a day in icy water with rain beating upon his head, heavy boulders to move and timbers to chop had worn him down. The high spirits of early June when he could not work had evaporated under the hard labor of late July. Yet hope ran high. He stayed.

Famous 1860 Placer Mines

Fergus refused to give up. Others like him, determined to make the fortune they came so far to seek, tucked into the heavy work and realized big rewards. Famous placer mines of the 1860s included George Mumford and company at Buffalo Flats (today's Breckenridge Golf Course); Daniel Stoggsdill's Kentucky workings at Delaware Flats (above Gold Run Gulch's mouth in the lower Swan River Valley); Leland Peabody and the Weaver boys in Gold Run (near the still-standing ruins of the Jessie Mill); J. A. Mower and Melcher Hangs' Stillson's Patch in lower French Gulch; John Sisler's placer in lower French Gulch; and productive placer claims in Negro or Nigger Gulch.

In that gulch discoverers included two blacks named Riddel and Jack. Together the five men hit a bonanza. According to the October 10, 1860 *Rocky Mountain News* they came with genuine need. One planned to buy his wife's freedom from her slave master with his gold:

> *"Nigger gulch" has paid well. We saw the Darkies after whom the gulch is named en route for the States, having taken out nearly $6,000 this season. One of them is graduate of Oberlin College. The other was a slave, but money purchased his freedom, he came here to seek money enough to buy his wife. Having accomplished his objective, he is now going to Independence, Mo. to pay the sum asked for her. For fear of being robbed, they sent their treasure by express.*

Nearby Towns Spring Up

Not only Breckenridge but also other camps sprang up like spring dandelions. During summer, 1860 every nearby gulch multiplied with wagons, log structures, shanties, tents and brush shelters. Shouts of men, braying of animals and mining cacophony filled the air. Green forest turned white with canvas: "For twelve miles on the river and from mouth to source of every gulch, skirts of timber are lined with the canvas of wagon covers and tents," the June 10, 1860 *Rocky Mountain News* declared.

Five new settlements burst into being in 1860:

Tiny *Buffalo Flats,* named for its view north to Buffalo Mountain, spread on the wide, flat valley of today's Breckenridge Golf Course in the Swan Valley. George Mumford, the camp's leading citizen, has descendants still living in Summit County. Mining observer Ovando J. Hollister in 1867 rated Buffalo Flats placer gold production higher than its gold-studded neighbor, Gold Run Gulch.

Busy *Delaware Flats* also lay in the Swan Valley near the mouth of rich Galena Gulch. It started small in 1859-60 with mostly tent dwellings. Later it housed the Langrishe & Dougherty theater and had the valley's second postoffice. Saloons, hotels and stores served a population that quadrupled in summer, 1861. Miners took out a steady $75 to $100 per day here, big money at the time.

Gilded *Parkville*, located on the South Fork of the Swan River below Georgia Pass (earlier called Swan River Pass) became the first county seat. The bustling burg had its own mint for coinage, its own brewery and thousands of residents who dined sumptuously on oysters and lobsters, strawberries and sparkling wine at the 1860 opening of the town's splendid Gayosa Hall. Georgia and nearby Humbug Gulches yielded fortunes in gold, sometimes $10,000 from one placer claim in a single summer.

Gold-seamed *Lincoln City* in French Gulch grew after Nate Weber

Lincoln City: Note town structures, upper right, in etching by roving artist.

overturned rich gold there on August 10, 1860, the Spaulding strike anniversary date. Unlike Buffalo Flats, Delaware City and Parkville, the town lasted through many decades. First named Paige City for an early resident, the town had the region's first school, opened by schoolmaster W. R. Pollack in 1862. Its location near the wire gold treasure trove on Farncomb Hill assured Lincoln City's permanence. Father John L. Dyer, the Colorado pioneer Snow Shoe Itinerant, built his cabin there in 1862.

Bloomfield, also called Quandary City, surrounded an August, 1860 silver lode strike near Hoosier Pass south of Breckenridge. Felix Poznansky discovered silver here. Prospectors on the Blue stampeded to the discovery of "Silver Lode," five miles above town, and excitedly staked out claims. Three hundred attended the first Peruvian Mining District meeting there. Assays of the silver rated its values sky high. And the silver's purity turned heads. Geologists surmised that the rich belt of silver predominant in the Montezuma area had resurfaced at Bloomfield where today's Monte Cristo Gulch and Monte Cristo Mine remain in ruins. Developers claimed a townsite named after J. M. Bloomfield and proposed giving away lots to anyone who would build.

Dr. E. H. Boyd, a prominent local leader who had an early claim in the Spaulding Diggings, became instrumental in establishing Bloomfield as a town. He later served as Summit County delegate to the Colorado Territorial Convention. Bloomfield, so early and so briefly in existence, remains shrouded by distant years.

Civil War Impacts Placer Mining

Miners continued to take out substantial amounts of free gold well into 1862. Then returns began to diminish as loose gold petered out. Summer 1862 saw reduced stream flow; miners could not wash their gold. In addition, the outbreak of the Civil War changed men's hearts.

Hard-working prospectors like Ezra Stahl, from Hartford City, Indiana, felt the tug of loyalty to home, state and country. Stahl, who according to his 1862 diary entries took out credible gold yields daily from his Delaware Flats claim, prepared to return home. Many followed his pattern. Before he left, the serious-minded and industrious young man indulged in a small fling. He paid several visits to the Delaware City's Langrishe & Dougherty melodrama theatre, including "The Miser of Marseilles." He reveled in each play. Toting a few tools, he then crossed the range to Hamilton near Tarryall, a town deserted by then, and weighed himself there—at all of 132 pounds. On Thursday, October 16, 1862 he arrived home. After visiting family and friends, Stahl, like so many other gold-seekers, enlisted in the Civil War.

During Ezra Stahl's three years around Breckenridge, the town took shape. Breckenridge boasted about 20 houses, many dirt-roofed, by mid-June 1860. Five or six business houses underway added to the two complete commercial buildings. The road from Tarryall flowed with men, pack animals, beef cattle, wagons and teams.

A *Western Mountaineer* correspondent using the pen name, Sea Pea,

O. A. Whittemore

gasped at the growth spurt during his one-week absence. "I hardly know the place," he wrote. Land forested a few weeks ago had given way to "stores, dwellings, shops and saloons." O. A. Whittemore started a store.

As late as May, 1860 William A. Smith noted that liquor had not yet made its way over the range. Now alcohol had arrived and saloons became a curious mix of comfortable miners' retreat, town hall where elections took place, meeting place for the Miners Court and a site for frontier-firebrand preaching of the gospel.

A sawmill opened, driving lumber prices down from a pricey $250 per thousand board feet to $150. Seventy-five to 100 inhabitants, including families, populated Breckenridge. Soon Breckenridge would wrestle the coveted county seat from Parkville, partly through intrigue, partly through attrition, as easy placer gold ran out. Now stores, hotels, saloons and a U.S. postoffice anchored the first town west of the Continental Divide in Colorado Territory.

Breckenridge, the new county seat, was born.

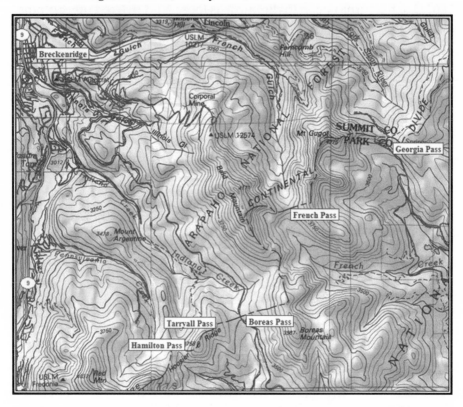

Parkville sprang up in 1860. New Georgia Pass, 11,598 feet, funneled traffic over the Snowy Range into that busy town. Sky-bumping French Pass, 12,057 feet, accommodated Lincoln-bound travelers. The new routes joined Tarryall and Hamilton, the 1859 gateways to Breckenridge. Boreas was used later.

(Author's Note: Hikers who want to experience the 1859 route, Tarryall Pass, can use *The New Summit Hiker*, Trail No. 7, "Indiana Creek." The saddle where hikers turn west to descend into Indiana Gulch is old Tarryall Pass.)

5

The 1870s

Tiny 1870 Breckenridge commanded the seat of government for a vast hinterlands which stretched north to the Wyoming border and west to the Utah line. The 1870s outpost, though its 1860 population had dwindled to a handful, enjoyed an oddball distinction: Breckenridge as county seat administered all of today's Grand, Routt, Eagle, Garfield, Moffat and Rio Blanco counties. No competitor challenged the county seat status; the frontier fiefdom remained the 14 million acre-Western Slope's governing capitol.

To rise to its noble calling, the 1870s town added several substantial log buildings and spruced up others with white-painted clapboard fronts. The fact that one local home builder unearthed a five-ounce gold nugget while digging his cellar didn't help the town image. Residents "stampeded" to Main Street, tore up the neighborhood and mined the gravel soil for gold. According to the September 4, 1874 *Rocky Mountain News*, they undermined the town buildings and left a notorious mess, including "heaps of rock and earth."

In one way, 1870s Breckenridge resembled Breckenridge a century later in its hippie-era 1970s. An unrelated family of locals stamped the town with a quirky identity. The 1874

1870s outpost governed huge territory.

News article depicted how nonconformist Breckenridge honored the Sabbath:

> The town—what there is of it—is scattered indiscriminately up the north bank of the Blue river, and looks as though it was dozing from the effects of a drunken spree. All of the trading, speculating, visiting, fighting and horse-racing, is performed on Sundays, the remainder of the week belong spent in the mines. A crazy, rickety frame building, which stands on the outskirts, and whose foundation has been partly washed away by a hydraulic ram in the universal search for gold, is used for a church, court-room, public hall, and all festive gatherings. Now and then a minister—generally of the Methodist persuasion—lands in Breckinridge, and, after treating the miners to a red-hot sermon on the evils of profanity and gambling, goes away freighted with gold dust and nuggets.

County government had replaced the swift justice of the Miners Court. (See the author's book, *Rascals, Scoundrels and No Goods*, for the spirited story of frontier justice in the 1860s Miners Court.) Sheriff A. L. Shock and district court judge Wells enforced territorial law. J. A. Willoughby served as county clerk, district court clerk, postmaster and as agent for Wells, Fargo and Company.

Stagecoach Travel

Breckenridge received mail three times weekly by stagecoach. The two-

Stagecoach lines carried mail and passengers over the Divide.

horse line operated by the Colorado Stage Company connected Breckenridge with Hamilton and the outside world. Fares ran about $2.50, nearly the miners' daily wage. Spottswood and Hogan had also transported mail and passengers over the range, a 17-mile trip in snappy Concord coaches. In winter drivers wore a long overcoat, sometimes buffalo fur, and a hat. They wrapped their feet in burlap to prevent slipping on ice. Drivers placed the lightest horses up front because they were least likely to cause snowslides. If an avalanche occurred, passengers helped to clear the track.

Travelers lodged at the Silverthorn Hotel ($9 - $13 for lodging per week and $7 for weekly board) and could purchase everything from bakery bread to miner's rubber boots in Breckenridge's log and shanty commercial core. Prices ran high: flour cost $10 a sack, coffee 33 cents a pound and sugar 23 cents. The August 14, 1872 *Rocky Mountain News* gave the retail report:

> As there is but one hotel—Mr. Silverthorn's—it of course is constantly crowded, and is one of the best paying enterprises here. There are four stores, all doing a fair business. The old firm of (James D.) Roby and Buens is selling a large amount of goods, and carrying on, besides, several profitable mines. Pitzer & Dickson, of Denver, are selling goods at this place. They carry a good stock of miners' supplies, and sell as fast as they can get them here. J. Fink has built and opened a clothing store, and is doing well. Charles Kahrhoff carries a fair stock of miners' goods, sells lager, gets all he can, and keeps what he gets. Schmitz & Rose carry on a bakery; sell bread, cakes and pies, and liquids to wash them down with. Fred D. Wolff supplies the miners with boots and shoes, and does the cobbling for all this district. J. W. Bombeck is the only butcher and his market wagon performs weekly rounds to the various camps and cabins for fifteen miles in every direction. G. H. Bressler is the city blacksmith, and the only one they have had here for a number of years; consequently he must be a good one.

Town Personalities

George Bressler, the able blacksmith, a pillar of Breckenridge society, caught the eye of a visiting lady journalist, Alice Polk Hill, who trilled about his handsome looks. Another observer remarked that Bressler played a fatherly role to the young miners, sometimes 20 packed nightly into his small cabin, who found themselves far from home and family. The village blacksmith, a vital necessity in a mining community, forged needed tools, hammered out horseshoes and fixed wagon wheels.

Bressler earned the town geniality award. But others shone also. The town's top snowshoer (the term used for skiing) was W.A. Davenport.

It's most energetic citizen was Will Iliff, the 1859er who came with Spaulding's party. Its steadiest, George Mumford, longtime county commissioner. Its gabbiest, John Shock, a storied conversationalist. The town's most distinguished resident was hunter, naturalist and taxidermist Edwin Carter, whose splendid collection of birds and animals of Colorado "made him a gentleman who does credit to the state and of whom Summit County is justly proud," the *News* said.

The town's most peculiar gent, the well-loved Judge Marshel Silverthorn, presided as 1860s judge of the Miners Court. The judge, a tiny bantam rooster of a man, was "dried to a crackling" and often doubled over into a hairpin of glee over a good joke.

Most popular lady was his wife, Agnes Ralston Silverthorn, a kindly and rotund woman, mother to the camp. The boys tramped with a sled over the top of Tarryall Pass each spring when she returned from Denver to Breckenridge. They made the climb to welcome their beloved Mrs. Silverthorn and pull her on the sled into town. Mrs. S., afraid of nothing, once shook down a squaw in Denver to retrieve a stolen sunbonnet. She ran feisty Chief Colorow from her hotel dining room when she tired of his demand for free biscuits.

The December 1, 1874 *Rocky Mountain News* commented:

> *Judge Silverthorn, as full of oddities and anecdotes as his good wife's larder is of the delicacies and necessaries of life, casts an approving eye on the prospects of the camp.*

Though this merry and offbeat assortment of Breckenridge personalities stamped the town character, a pall hung over the former mining beehive. Gone were the days when 5,000 frenzied gold seekers flooded nearby Parkville, when hotels and saloons rose in a single night. Also gone also were the coffee cans of gold nuggets that anchored wooden tables in Gold Run Gulch cabins. Down from $2,000 and $3,000 weekly cleanups of the early 1860s, 1870s miners rarely extracted a tenth of that amount. Individual miners lacked the cash to put in the proper machinery and water power to make their claims pay.

Gold remained plentiful. It salted, seamed and latticed the ground. The 1859-62 rush had only skimmed the surface. A few men, including reporter, C. J. Reid, recognized that only manpower, money and machines could harvest the wealth locked in the land. He prophesied in the September 4, 1874 *Rocky Mountain News*:

> *No systemized effort has yet been made to reach the bed-rock in the valley, and these rich fields stand to this day unclaimed. Here is an opportunity for enterprise and capital, and a big dividend for any company that will take hold of it.*

Enter Thomas H. Fuller.

This prosperous Boston businessman strode onto the Summit County scene in 1868. He possessed the savvy to see Breckenridge's mining potential in a new way and he had the money to finance its development. Fuller's annual income, recorded in the 1870 census, reached $50,000, then a tidy sum. He also had the influence to raise capital from investors.

Fuller observed that placer mining's key requirement lay in the need for water. Miners' success came at the mercy of a just-right stream flow—not too heavy as in spring runoff and not too light as in drought summers or dry autumn months. He wanted to introduce high-pressure hydraulic methods to wash gold from gulch sides with giant water streams.

Breckenridge miners pioneered hydraulic mining in Colorado. Men were "tearing up 'Mother Nature' at an alarming rate," the Miners Record noted.

So Thomas Fuller embarked on a water project of such magnitude for 1870 that it stuns the imagination. What came from the effort, after years of work and administrative change, was an 1870s mining wonder: the Great Flume.

Fuller purchased and took over claims in the incredibly-rich gulches around old Parkville—Georgia, American and Humbug. He also bought claims in Illinois and Mayo gulches. He snapped up obscure hillside patches and new gorges and ravines previously untouched. He purchased the water rights. He had a plan.

As Fuller accomplished this, another man, Augustus Greenleaf, carried out the same kind of acquisition in the same area. Instead of viewing one another as competitors, they combined their efforts in one company. Fuller formed a partnership with Augustus Greenleaf on June 16, 1871 launching the Fuller & Greenleaf Mining and Ditch Company.

The *Rocky Mountain News*, August 8, 1872, stated, "The most extensive mining company in this district (Breckenridge) is Fuller & Greenleaf; they are working over a hundred men." It took a portable company town to maintain these workers.

Steel-reinforced wooden reservoir for Great Flume, fed by a 2-mile waterway from Little French Creek, provided water for American and Georgia Gulches.

Together they brought water to their placer ground, transporting it from sources high up so that it possessed the driving force necessary for the hydraulic gulch-washing that used huge hoses and nozzles. They planned to start by gouging gulch banks and washing the dirt to retrieve money metal from the gold-laced ground around and above once-rich Parkville. Early miners failed to exhaust its storied riches.

They purchased three major water conduits developed by the early prospectors:

1. the 6.5-mile long American Ditch, built by 1860 prospectors to carry water from the South Swan River just below Georgia Pass to upper Georgia Gulch.

2. the eight-mile Stevens Flume, built by 1861 miners to bring water from the Middle Swan River to rich American and Dry gulches.

3. the two-mile Pollard Ditch built in 1861 to transport water from the South Swan to the lower part of Georgia Gulch near old Parkville.

To these Fuller gradually added,

4. the Swan River and Georgia Gulch Flume. From 1871 to 1876 it grew to 14 miles and served American and Georgia gulches. This wooden flume, built solid to handle a huge amount of water, measured four feet wide at its bottom, six feet wide at its cantilevered top and stood a full six feet tall. Its amazing capacity was over 1.6 million gallons of water per hour.

Along the way, Fuller shed his partner, Greenleaf. He formed the Fuller Placer Company, incorporated on September 25, 1875. Then he constructed,

5. the Mount Guyot Flume. This innovative project took water from a high lake on the Atlantic side of Georgia Pass across the Continental Divide and carried it to the Pacific side. This trans-Divide flume, completed in 1876, then stood as the world's only diversion from the Atlantic watershed to the Pacific.

*A **flume** is a raised, wooden water conduit, a trough or a pipe, undergirded by supports and trestles.*

So by the end of 1876 Fuller had five major flumes and ditches: the American Ditch, the Stevens Flume, the Pollard Ditch, the Swan River and Georgia Gulch Flume and the Mount Guyot Flume. These, along with smaller ditches and feeders which drew from streams the flumes and ditches crossed, totaled a staggering 50 miles in length. The grand achievement earned the accolade "The Great Flume."

Though it cost a substantial $100,000, the Great Flume put Fuller's property on America's mining map. It serviced Fuller's five square miles of selected mineral lands east of Breckenridge. In a few short years, Thomas H. Fuller had acquired mining land and developed it to outdistance all other placer operations in the state of Colorado. His workings surpassed every other east of California, according to early mining book authors George Crofutt and Frank Fossett.

Fuller's innovation continued as the first in Summit County to use

As early as 1861, Parkville miners petitioned the Territorial Legislature to charter the Stevens Flume. Built at that time, it later became part of Thomas Fuller's Great Flume, shown here on the Swan River's Middle Fork.

Giants, kind of oversized fire hose. *The Engineering and Mining Journal*, August 18, 1877 remarked,

> *The Fuller Company, who is operating on a larger scale than any other organization in the valley, have 6 Giants at work, and are taking out from $3,000 to $5,000 per week, at an expense of $1,500. This company will produce as much this year as was taken out of the entire valley last year.*

The *Journal*'s December 22, 1877 article described profits poured back into the endeavor:

> *From (1871) onward, Col. Fuller and the company that bears his name have been steadily accumulating ground, buying up segregated claims, preempting new gulches and patches, and perfecting its water system, until, at the present date, it is one of the largest placer mining organizations in the State, and, so far as development is concerned, far in advance of any other.*

Ruins Still Remain

Physical remnants of four sawmills along the fourteen-mile-route of the Swan River and Georgia Gulch flume exist today. One is an original built by Fuller. The other three, located in Bull, Missouri and Days gulches, went up 20 years after Fuller. They provided boards for an 1890s property owner, the Wapiti Mining Company, to rebuild part of Fuller's 20-year old flume. Discovered by field researcher, Bill Fountain, the remains evidence the massive amount of sawed lumber (two million

Ruins of one of four sawmills constructed to supply 2 million feet of lumber to rebuild Fuller's flume in the 1890s.

feet for the 14-mile flume) needed for construction of the flume, its supports and trestles. Workers built sawmills and installed sawmill equipment on site. These sawmills turned out ten thousand feet of lumber in 24 hours, with all the lumber cut and the timbers ready to put into the flume. Supervisors hired and trained men. Teams of horses, wagons, equipment and loggers worked to cut and then transport the logs to the sawmills and the finished planks to their destination. They filled the gulches with noise and dust. Managers oversaw construction and purchasing for boarding houses, kitchens, outhouses and equipment for the workmen. Laborers cut the flume's grade and removed trees. Carpenters, probably several teams of them, rebuilt the flume.

Mining authority Frank Fossett, in his 1879 *Colorado, Its Gold and Silver Mines*, predicted a stunning level of success for Thomas H. Fuller's endeavor, an $8 million total output:

> *Last year the gold product was reported at $42,000, and expenses at $15,000. The yield for 1879, the present summer and fall, may reach $100,000, as everything is now in first-class condition. Six Little Giant hydraulics are at work in different gulches. There are all together about 34,0000 cubic yards of pay gravel, capable of yielding twenty-five cents per cubic yard, indicating the total contents to exceed $8,000,000.*

Historian Fossett also published yield figures for Summit County gold placers through 1878. Starting in 1876 when the Great Flume stood complete, placer production doubled. Gold yield in 1874 totaled $76,408 and in 1875, $72,413. But in 1876 and 77, total yield rises to $150,000, and in 1878 climbs to $165,774. Placer mining enhanced by the Great Flume clearly boosted profits.

Fuller's trend-setting consolidation of mining properties left the area with less than a dozen individual placer mine owners by 1879, according to the June 1, 1880 *Breckenridge Mining Gazette,* a one-time promotional publication.

The brilliant success of the Fuller Placer Company attracted buyers. In 1880, the Summit County Mining and Smelting Company (SCMSC) purchased Fuller company assets. Through various owners, the Fuller properties played a stellar role in Breckenridge mining history, producing high yields of gold over legendary decades. SCMSC later sold to the Victoria Gold Mining Company, which became the storied Wapiti Mining Company. Owned by magnate John Campion, Wapiti was managed by mining mogul and dredge king, Ben Stanley Revett. Fuller's property became a legacy.

Wooden cribbing which supported the flume, remains today.

PIONEER PROFILE: Colonel Thomas H. Fuller

Bostonian Thomas Fuller gained his initial wealth from the manufacture of nails—not just any nails but horseshoe nails. And not ordinary horseshoe nails but what the January 8, 1876 *Rocky Mountain News* called "the best horse nails in the world, using the very highest grades of Swedish iron." Fuller's nails earned medals at state fairs. They won contracts from the U.S. government's war department. Consumers and dealers "from all over the civilized world" flocked orders to Fuller's Globe Nail Company. His company employed 150 men in Boston and produced five tons of nails daily—but failed to keep up with demand.

First as principal stockholder and treasurer of Boston's Globe Nail Company and later as its president, Thomas H. Fuller made good money.

But he had a brilliance beyond the predictable nail business. A creative thinker, and bold innovator, he excelled at being an entrepreneur. Behind his business-like manner, Fuller concealed a hunger for challenge.

Many Americans who longed to test their mettle on the frontier went west. Thomas Fuller traveled to the Colorado mountains for his health in the late 1860s and ended up testing his mettle.

As he recuperated in Breckenridge, Fuller saw opportunity. Instead of abandoned ground littered by mining debris, he saw land with golden treasure hidden but accessible below its bleak surface. That ground, gleaned by shallow mining with little expertise and less equipment, now waited. Fuller heard a whisper audible on the cutting edge of the wind, "Now!"

Thomas Fuller had long drowned his calling in a pool of duty. Born in Enosbury, Vermont in 1815, he remained with his parents and worked as a merchant till his late 30s. He never married. Perhaps upon his parents' deaths, he moved to Boston to become a partner from 1852-54 with a West India goods dealer, Hayward, French and Fuller. The firm shifted to groceries during the recession years of 1855-59 under a new name, French, Fuller and Fogg. By 1867, Fuller had moved to the nail manufacturing business he managed till 1882.

Abruptly his world changed. Commuting by rail and stagecoach from Boston, Fuller in 1868 launched his life of adventure. His innovation transformed Breckenridge mining.

Though untrained as an engineer, Fuller had the savvy to recognize that a lake above 11,841-foot Georgia Pass could provide a reliable source of water for placer claims serviced by the ambitious new flume. For the first time—and the only time—Fuller caused Atlantic watershed water to flow through a Continental Divide pass for use on the Pacific side. He provided an innovative solution to placer mining's biggest problem.

First in Summit County to use Little Giants to wash hillsides to retrieve their ancient gold deposits, first to build extensive flumes and ditches, first to command capital to fund a large mining company, Thomas H. Fuller was a cutting-edge thinker and mining visionary.

Thomas H. Fuller continued to increase his impressive holdings through 1879. He then ranked as head of the largest mining operation in Colorado and one of the largest in the West.

At the height of his mining career in 1879, Thomas Fuller's health declined. His struggle with his unknown malady forced him to leave his Breckenridge mining venture behind and return to Boston for medical care.

The illness that took his life at first sapped his energy. Failing in strength, Summit's greatest mine consolidator in February, 1880 traded his holdings to Summit County Mining and Smelting Company, probably for reimbursement in stock, according to his biographical researcher, Bill Fountain. Sadly, that stock proved worthless in a year's time. Fuller's estate failed to benefit from his mining achievement because of poor management and huge stock losses by SCMSC, a company whose assets at Fuller's passing had already seen liquidation at sheriff's sales. Nevertheless, Fuller's net worth at his death on March 3, 1882 stood at nearly $115,000, a healthy sum. $25,000 of that went to Philomela Cole, the wife of Fuller's able company superintendent, who cared for him in Boston's Union Park until his death. A reduced amount went to a sister and the rest to charity.

Fuller's impact on mining trends cannot be measured. He stands among the first U.S. mining leaders to perceive that only large, well-financed, organized mining companies could exploit placer deposits. The day of the independent miner had ended.

Fuller led the way when he bought and consolidated a multitude of claims into a mega-company.

He was Summit County's first mining magnate. He ranks with dredge king Ben Stanley Revett, who would, decades later, manage Fuller's properties for the Wapiti Mining Company. Thomas H. Fuller looms large on the Colorado mining horizon.

Researcher Bill Fountain discusses hydraulic mining in American Gulch. He discovered remains of the 1870s Great Flume and walked its entire route.

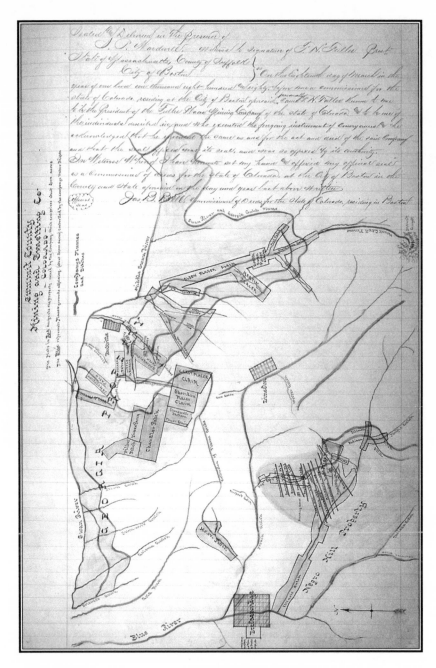

This detailed 1880 map accompanied legal documents which conveyed an ailing Thomas Fuller's extensive placer and lode claims, plus water rights and buildings, to Summit County Mining and Smelting Co.

6

The 1880s

B reckenridge, an insignificant colony holed up on the frontier, braced for change. The first rumble in a coming earthquake emitted from a cry of "Eureka!" by Will Iliff. He's the 1859er who took $7,000 from his claim near Spaulding's August 10, 1859 discovery.

Iliff's early luck held. In 1878, prompted by news of gold veins in hard rock at nearby Leadville, he struck gold at the Blue Danube lode mine. After this landmark discovery, other new strikes followed, like waves of aftershock.

A new gold rush began, this time in lode mining. By 1879 Breckenridge experienced cataclysmic change.

Area population shot from 250 to 2,000. Lots priced at $25 skyrocketed to $1,500. Construction of 500 new buildings between February and May 1880 fueled the town economy and filled the streets with joyful racket. Loggers hacked down town pine groves that earlier shaded a generation of placer miners, creating a sea of stumps. Three large sawmills ran day and night, according to the *Breckenridge Mining Gazette*, a promotional publication dated June 1, 1880. One hundred mining companies organized. Prospectors filed 6,190 location certificates.

"Carpenters hammers never stopped day or night," wrote a sleepless Agnes Miner, granddaughter of old Judge Silverthorn. An equally exhausted Methodist minister, Father John Lewis Dyer, moaned, "The weary could hardly rest."

Hubbub came not only from round-the-clock construction but also from 18 saloons, three dance halls and a bevy of gambling halls. Hurdygurdy music flowed into the streets and shouts from saloon carousers split the air. The quiet Breckenridge of 1870s placer mining days was gone. And so, largely, was placer mining. Hardrock mining seized the day.

The *Rocky Mountain News* on May 16, 1880 detailed the boom:

The town is growing so rapidly at present that a description noted to-day would not be true of to-morrow. Lots have advanced twelve hundred per centum in value since the beginning of the year, and some of the most prominent owners still look for better rates. To the casual observer the town and town property is pushing ahead of the mines, and, if the present rate of increase lasts for a month, will have to await developments in the shafts and at the smelters. New buildings and tents are going up on every side. Streets are being cleared among the hill side pines, while the sixty or more arrivals each day are many of them engaged in providing for themselves in temporary structures or abandoned log huts.

The lode mining boom transformed log-cabin Breckenridge (inset) to a Victorian town with churches (far l. and r.) and schoolhouse (center l.).

Town Transformation

A dizzied Breckenridge town government sought to incorporate the bulging burg. They did so on March 3, 1880. In April, voters elected town trustees. Officials reacted to a scathing editorial from the town's new newspaper, the *Breckenridge Daily Journal,* by clearing Main Street of boulders and filling in "cellar-sized holes." They yanked abandoned cabins from their haphazard location in the middle of streets. They stripped ragged tents and skeleton buildings from Ridge Street, slated to shine as Breckenridge's showiest 1880s thoroughfare.

The 1880s transformed Breckenridge from log and shanty 1860s architecture to a Victorian jewel. The age of Britain's Queen Victoria had ushered in building design featuring false fronts, gingerbread trim and unrestrained propriety. The pretentiousness of Victorian social principles proved as artificial as its structural false fronts. For example, prim parlor etiquette reigned side by side with licensed houses of prostitution. The ill-starred attempt to control the untamed boom town with the constraint of Victorian virtue produced amusing results—like squashing a fat lady into a whalebone corset. Something was bound to pop. Breckenridge's sporting element ignored the rules to indulge in carousing. The era of contrast has left Breckenridge a heritage of gem Victorian buildings in a treasured National Historic District.

PIONEER PROFILE: William H. Iliff

Will Iliff participated in the discovery strike of Breckenridge's two big gold rushes, the initial strikes which set off the two booms of 1859 and 1880—a real distinction.

Iliff stood with Spaulding on August 10, 1859 and quickly made his own bigger find nearby. Iliff himself precipitated the 1880 boom by striking the gold vein that launched the lode mining rush.

Born January 4, 1836 in Perry, Ohio of British descent, Iliff arrived in Denver on July 6, 1859. For this he ranks as a Colorado Pioneer. The 23-year old joined the 1859 Lawrence party headed for Blue River. Digging only ten feet deep, he quickly retrieved that storied $7,000 in gold from his claim neighboring Spaulding's.

Success crowned Iliff's efforts. But he didn't sit back. By late August he had volunteered to make the arduous—and dangerous—trek to Denver to purchase supplies for the Spaulding miners. James Mitchell and "Cucumber" (who gave his name to Cucumber Gulch) joined him. Before he left, he panned some pocket gold to show off. Everyone wanted to buy it. The high-quality gold earned him $18 per ounce in Denver (the going rate: $16) and touched off a stampede to the Blue.

However, when Civil War broke out in 1861, Iliff returned to Perry, Ohio to enlist in the 12th Ohio Volunteer Infantry on June 15. He remained in uniform till July 11, 1864. He came back to Breckenridge and had his name listed in the 1870 census there.

Reports of hardrock discoveries in 1878 drew him to Leadville. Ever the mining student, he observed and learned the ways of lode mining. On his return, he prospected his own Breckenridge "back yard." He unearthed a 10-foot crevice of gold ore that Iliff named the Blue Danube. The April 6, 1880 *Rocky Mountain News* recorded the discovery strike:

William H. Iliff, who had examined the formation at Leadville, returned and in company with George H. Bressler, commenced prospecting on the west bank of the Blue, now known as Shock hill . . . This was named the Blue Danube, and is notable as the pioneer discovery of the district.

Iliff's Blue Danube set off the earthquake that jerked sleepy Breckenridge awake. When the town incorporated and elected a municipal government in April, 1880, Will Iliff joined trustees James Whitstone, James D. Roby, George H. Bressler, Samuel De-Matte and Peter Engle. They in turn selected him to be board president and mayor.

In 1884, Iliff ran for sheriff and won, serving until 1886. Like everyone else in town, he also mined. At his 7:30 Mine a mile below Boreas Pass on Bald Mountain's south slope, he built a large boardinghouse in 1883, plus a shaft house and bunk house. The mine had a highly-visible ore tram that stretched its way up Baldy's grassy slope. Despite Iliff's sizeable investment the mine earned little until 1893 when new strikes carried it into the 20th century.

The mine bore the name 7:30 for the time work began. But tardy miners caused management to throw up their hands and change the name—to 7:40.

Once he got here, Will Iliff put down roots he refused to take up. He lasted longer in Breckenridge than any other local 1859er. The inveterate miner Iliff never married. He died in Buena Vista at age 66 with no descendants. Yet he left an inheritance to Breckenridge history. Though little recognized, his impact on the town's heritage deserves honor.

While town life prospered, miners in nearby gulches faced a problem. Hardrock ore cost them a fortune to freight. They had to ship their ore to mills for crushing. Miners and mining companies buckled under the wagon hauling rates. But teamsters made good money. The May 16, 1880 *Rocky Mountain News* added details on construction and living costs:

Laborers are in demand, especially those with teams, who are making from $12 to $15 per day. Prices are fixed in the grocery line at about twenty per cent above eastern rates. Native lumber is $40 per thousand, shingles $6, nails fifteen cents per pound, etc. Day board is $7 to $9 per week. Meals are fifty cents. Hotel rates are $2 to $3 per day. The through fare from Denver is $11.80.

Narrow Gauge Railway

Mine owners, whose high ore freight costs ate up part of their profits, awaited relief. It occurred with another rumble in the 1880s earthquake, the coming of the railroad. In 1881, the gutsy narrow gauge railway started by Colorado Governor John Evans pushed its grueling way from Como up Boreas Pass. In fall, 1882 the Denver, South Park & Pacific Railroad chugged into Breckenridge, its shiny black locomotive gleaming in the sun and its steam engine belching a white plume of prosperity.

For prosperity had come with Breckenridge's bustling 1880s. Mine owners' freight costs plummeted with the railroad's lower ore freight charges. Merchants received luxury goods to satisfy the demands of residents growing rich in the mines. Side pork and sourdough, oatmeal, tinned fruit, hardtack and tea gave way to tables loaded with biscuits and butter, eggs, thick slabs of ham, pitchers of cream and the occasional luxury of a fresh orange. Oysters and champagne began to appear on the menus of Breckenridge's ten restaurants.

The railroad put South Park-Breckenridge stagecoach lines out of business. During rail-building days, J. Spottswood's Pioneer Stage Company transported passengers up the range daily to connect with the advancing railroad. On rail completion, that service ended. Local stage lines still flourished. They shuttled passengers and mail to new 1880s-born towns such as Preston, Swan City and also Lincoln, an 1860s town.

The coming railroad also eliminated use of the 1859ers' route, Tarryall Pass. The Continental Divide pass at 11,488 feet, took the new name of Boreas. Rail officials first chose the name Spottswood after the stageline company. They later settled on a new name, after the ancient Greek god of the wind, Boreas. This name prevailed. A rail depot community at the pass summit also bore the name Boreas.

Mining Jackpot

Breckenridge marked its biggest mining year ever in 1881. In a decade when 75 cents bought a sumptuous dinner, the region yielded over $1.5 million.

All through the 1880s, Breckenridge mines dazzled Colorado and the nation. Successive waves of discoveries included Farncomb Hill with its jewelry-quality wire gold nuggets . . . mineral-laced Swan Valley with

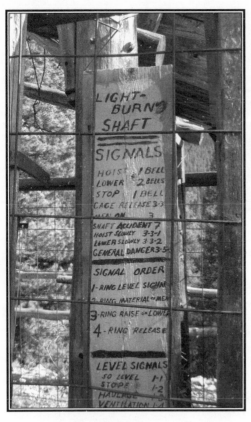

A complex set of Lightburn shaft signals guides the hoist man, warns of danger.

its gold-rich Cashier and IXL mines . . . Gold Run Gulch's Jessie and Jumbo . . . French Gulch, seamed with gold, zinc and lead, home to famous mines like the Country Boy and the Oro-Wellington . . . Illinois Gulch's impressive Washington Mine . . . Boreas' 7:40 and Warriors Mark . . . the rich Monte Cristo (new name for the old Quandary Lode at Bloomfield), Senator and Bemrose Placer on Hoosier Pass.

In French Gulch John Sisler employed dozens of men at his Sisler Placer on the Lincoln Road. As each man sat down to nightly supper, he received his day's wages beside his tin plate in the form of gold dust taken from the mine that day.

New prospectors who poured into the town fanned out into the hills and gulches to discover gold. New mine camps and towns sprouted during the 1880s:

Braddocks, took the name of its colorful leading citizen, Broncho Dave Braddocks. Located on the west side of today's Highway 9 just south of Tiger Road, the town touted Dave's high altitude vegetable farm, his popular temperance beer, his lavish parties staged in an 1882-built hall. The *Montezuma Millrun,* like everyone else, loved to see Dave coming. "His wagon was full of beer and cider and his soul full of fun." Dave ran a stage line to Preston and Swan City. When the railroad established a depot at Braddocks, it became a receiving station for Swan Valley ores.

Preston, launched by John Shock in 1875, came into its own in the 1880s. It perched on Gibson Hill where the rich Jumbo and Buffalo claims caused a prospector stampede to the town. Shock managed the Preston boardinghouse. Its neighbors included a rarity—a fruit and vegetable market— and a bonus for ladies, a dressmaking shop.

Swan City, located at the mouth of mineral-rich Brown's Gulch, sprang up in May, 1880 when miners discovered ore assayed at $800 to the ton. By August, Swan City had a postoffice, store, hotel and Dickson's Saloon. The historic Cashier and IXL mines boosted town growth. Mining-season population grew to 300 by 1886.

Rexford, a company town in the early 1880s, provided a civilized collection of general store, assay office, saloon, boardinghouse-hotel, postoffice and company headquarters for officials, lode miners and mill workers of the Rexford Mine Company.

Conger, later called Argentine, lay on the old stagecoach-wagon road in Indiana Gulch. Founded in 1880 by Colonel Sam Conger, it hosted a sawmill, ore mill, stores and 30-40 cabins. Its postoffice operated only until 1883.

Dyersville, named for Colorado pioneer preacher and Snow Shoe Itinerant, Father John Lewis Dyer, also clustered along the wagon-stagecoach road, near the minister's silver-studded Warriors Mark Mine. The town, planned to be his retirement retreat, had a saloon nearby, the Angel's Rest—which gave saintly Father Dyer no rest.

Farnham, below the Boreas Pass summit, occupied a magnificent mountain slope with plans for a 16-room resort hotel.

Boreas, the summit rail depot enclave, later had the nation's highest U.S. postoffice, which straddled the Continental Divide at 11,488 feet. The Denver, South Park & Pacific station had a five room, one and one-half story section house (still standing), an 1884 stone engine house with turntable, office, telegraph room, water tank, huge coal bin and 600-foot long covered snowshed, which made the depot area very dark.

With railroad service came the telegraph. Breckenridge enjoyed the convenience of its telegraph office located on Main Street until rail officials moved it west of the Blue to the depot in 1884, a "decided inconvenience at one-half mile from town." The *Journal,* predicting a barrage of cuss words from telegraph customers, pinpointed the love-hate relationship a future Breckenridge would continue to have with its railroad.

Early Harpers Illustrated Weekly writers traveled with artists who created etchings for readers. In the 1880s photographers took over.

A New Town Persona

As money metal flowed from area mines and mine camps into the coffers of town government and business, Breckenridge assumed new prestige. According to the January 1, 1884 *Rocky Mountain News*, this prosperous little city boasted "well laid out streets, fine business blocks and cozy residences . . . comfortable hotels, numerous churches and creditable schools with a population that averages in culture and refinement with the best anywhere."

The reason for all that culture? Women. They had come to Breckenridge to stay. As late as the 1870s, many wives blew out of Breckenridge with the first winter wind. They returned in May. Now women lived in their Breckenridge homes year round. They lobbied for schools. Gifted Victorian architect Elias Nashold designed a $5,000 two-story Victorian schoolhouse for 134 pupils on Harris Street in 1882. Women pushed for churches. St. Mary's Catholic Church, St. John's Episcopal and Father Dyer Methodist Church arose to meet the need. They introduced evening entertainments, sewing circles and musical performances. Breckenridge in 1880 boasted the Havens & Company opera and music hall, complete with an orchestra and plans for private box seating in its rear-of-the-building theater. Women also started enterprises. Mrs. J.W. Remine, who had earlier operated a boardinghouse, opened her resplendent European Hotel to an admiring populace in 1880.

Breckenridge's first suicide, a woman, occurred during this cultural growth spurt. Dolly Lane, a dance-house girl, took an overdose of morphine. Her death, the newspaper remarked, "temporarily hushed" the hurdy-gurdy music that poured from dance hall windows.

A maturing Breckenridge welcomed its first bank with pride. The Bank of Breckenridge, launched with ample working reserves of $30,000, resided in a new two-story frame building at the Ridge and Lincoln corner. The structure, constructed so it could be entirely enclosed with brick or stone for added surety, housed a first class vault and five-ton safe. However, none of these protections could guard the bank's funds from the ineptitude or larceny of its officers and directors. By Christmas, 1882, the three-year old Bank of Breckenridge had failed. The December 23, 1882 *Montezuma Millrun* labeled the institution "a miserable apology for a bank" and charged it of accepting $18,000 from depositors 48 hours before the bank closed.

Breckenridge's earlier disasters were not financial but natural ones. In June, 1880 Breckenridge's able-bodied men had responded to a ravaging forest fire by forming a bucket brigade of 100 men to stem the blaze. A merciful rain quenched the fire, which threatened to engulf the town in its fury. Forest fires had plagued Breckenridge from its earliest days when careless 1859-60 prospectors caused blaze after blaze, transforming the primeval pine forest into a distasteful miles-wide stand of blackened trunks.

A dozen wagons, the first on sled runners, advance on wintry Main Street. Fire hall, with bell tower, moved from French St. in late 1880s.

This time the near-disaster prompted the formation of a fire department. The town moved with unmatched speed to construct a $1,864 firehouse by July 13 following the June blaze. Located next to famous "Snow Shoe Itinerant" Father John Lewis Dyer's Methodist church (and dwarfing that humble house of worship), the firehouse proudly displayed a big, loud bell. On Sunday mornings, the preacher climbed the bell tower and sent the clanging bell's summons throughout the town. Sleepy firemen joined those more accustomed to Father Dyer's fiery preaching for a rousing Sunday sermon.

Future fires would devastate Breckenridge. Just two years later, according to the August 1, 1882 *Rocky Mountain News,* a Main Street fire destroyed A. LaCour's French bakery, D. B. Carpenter's jewelry store and a Chinese wash house.

"Celestials"

Notice that the Chinese business owner is unnamed. Asians, called "celestials," received little welcome in 1880s Breckenridge. Colorado leaders John Evans and Horace Tabor had sponsored Chinese immigration as a source of cheap mine labor. The largest colony of Chinese outside Denver, 400 men, resided nearby in Como. When the Chinese filtered over the Divide to Breckenridge, they received a rude reception.

The May 18, 1880 *Rocky Mountain News* reported,

The advent of a lot of chinamen into Breckenridge Sunday afternoon caused an indignation meeting of the miners on the following evening in which it was resolved that "the heathen must go." Accordingly the miners as soon as the meeting had closed, marched in a body to the habitations of the obnoxious element, notifying each one that they must not be seen in the place after 5 O'clock p.m. Tuesday night.

One Asian, Choy the Chinese laundry owner, enjoyed unusual favor in 1880s Breckenridge. His building, still standing at 107 North Main, went up in the early 1860s, a broad-ax log structure faced with lap siding to dress up the front façade. Choy mastered the art of customer relations, giving his clients hand-embroidered silk handkerchiefs as Chinese New Year gifts and filling their children's hands with candy and Chinese nuts. Choy's workers, displaying their long pigtails, dressed in black satin suits and caps as they picked up customers' laundry.

Breckenridge proved its loyalty to Choy when a trickster passed the laundryman a $10 Confederate note and received seven good U.S. dollars in change. Defending Choy, citizens ran the schemer out of town.

Pioneer Barney Ford, an escaped slave, mastered his own destiny as a miner, restaurateur, hotel owner and civic leader.

Choy's story illustrates the duality of Breckenridge's social structure. The affluent patronized the town's growing list of fine hotels—the Grand Central (H.R. Danenhower, proprietor), Arlington (J.P. Ecklund, prop.), Carbonate, Denver House (H.C. Grant, prop), Merchant's, National and Union hotels. The well-fixed also popularized black pioneer Barney Ford's restaurant. "Mr. Ford has introduced the California style chop house," the *Mining Gazette* noted, "which meets with great favor."

Mine laborers probably dined at lesser establishments than Ford's They earned less money in the 1880s than during the 1860s. In 1864-65 workers took home an average $4 to $5 per day. In 1879, that wage dropped to $2 to $2.50 per day. However, the sky-high prices of the early days plunged with increased availability of food and supplies.

Early 1880s: Finding's Hardware, below "Groceries" sign, burned in 1884.

Daily Life

An 1887 expense list, found in a decaying cloth bag along with a Civil War medal and Heidsieck champagne-flavored tobacco, illustrates a price drop from the 1860s. The miner, named Thomas, lists:

bread	.25	candles	.25
apples	.25	washtub	1.65
syrup	.75	looking glass	.50
sausage	.25	padlock	.35

Breckenridge area residents like Thomas faced a challenge living through the 1880s—cold winters. An August 31, 1882 snowstorm had dumped 18 inches of summer snow on Breckenridge. That was just the start of the Denver, South Park & Pacific's first winter of rail service, 1882-83. That season unleashed a fury of heavy snow and high winds, stopping the trains on their tracks. A few years later, on December 21, 1887, for example, the deep freeze outdoors measured -20 degrees before midnight and plunged to -42 degrees at 4 a.m. When their best whiskey froze, saloon keepers knew it was cold!

These cool facts would be lost without the advent of newspaper journalism in 1880s Breckenridge. The *Breckenridge Daily Journal*, which later became the *Summit County Journal*, debuted July 22, 1880. Its feisty editor, Jonathan Cooper Fincher, wielded both a sharp quill pen and unparalleled power in the community. Town fathers' heads jerked when Fincher railed about refuse, glassware and bailing wire that littered Main Street. They cleaned it up. Fincher fended off competitors, including the rival *Summit County Leader* which had the brass to launch publication 10 days after Fincher's first *Journal* edition. He labeled the *Leader's* two-man editorial team "a fool and a liar."

He may have lacked the crust to also demean Colorado's first newspaper woman, Kitty Hardy McAdoo. Daughter of *Summit County Leader* editor Charles Hardy, she wrote and edited news stories. Wife of leading townsman, William McAdoo, she also produced 11 children, successfully combining motherhood and career well ahead of her time.

Breckenridge Daily Journal (left) published 1880-1888 under editer Fincher. Melting spring snows encourage men and three ladies to shop on Main St.

Despite Fincher's abuse, the *Leader* managed to last 12 years. The *Journal*, in its several iterations, has lasted 130 years and still appears today.

A modern-day newspaper editor, the *Washington Post's* Ben Bradlee, said, "News is the first draft of history." Recording history, Breckenridge's newspapers, the *Journal, Leader, Democrat, Bi-Metallic, Bulletin,*

Miner, Herald, Star and Gazette, wrote that first draft. They bragged up Breckenridge, became incensed about politics, glowed over mining prospects and mourned the town's tragedies. They announced in 1882 the town's new cemetery. They heralded in 1887 the discovery of Colorado's largest gold nugget, Tom's Baby, in Breckenridge's Gold Flake Tunnel. Today the brittle pages of remaining copies, cracked and yellowed along the page edges, evoke memories of fancy dress balls, workers maimed by explosives, arrival of the first motor car, awe over 1900s capitalists. Headlines proclaimed everything from two world wars to a girls' berry-picking expedition.

Colorado's most colorful narrow gauge, the Denver, South Park & Pacific, provided passengers with views. Here, Ten Mile peaks from Boreas Pass.

7

The 1890s

Affluent 1890s Breckenridge ushered in an era of social elegance.

Victorian Breckenridge came into its own in the glittering 1890s. Fancy balls, with the ladies in ostrich feather boas, elegant brocades and jewels crowned the social year. Sprigged flower wallpapers, parlor parties and calling cards came to Breckenridge. The days of pioneer women stirring soup over a cast-iron cookstove while reading newspapers glued to rough log walls disappeared forever.

The prosperous 1890s decade stands out for its bounty of gold nuggets. Headline after newspaper headline touted the discoveries of large single nuggets, stashes of nuggets, caches of nuggets, nuggets hanging by a strand of gold wire, nuggets like candy cupped in a golden bowl. Bob Foote bumped his head on a rock projecting from a tunnel ceiling. Muttering, he took out the offending rock to discover a treasure trove of nuggets behind it. Headlines as far away as the *Chicago Tribune* heralded a pocket of gold on Farncomb Hill which "contained $10,000 in nuggets and a sort of free lace gold." This became known as Farncomb Hill wire gold.

But the showstopper had appeared just before the decade began. On July 23, 1887, Colorado's largest gold nugget dazzled the eyes of its discoverers. Tom Groves and Harry Litton unearthed it in the Gold Flake Tunnel, a Victoria Mining Company property. The jumbo "baby" weighed 156 ounces after cleaning and removal of considerable loose gold. This began a gold-nugget good-luck streak that stretched through the 1890s. According to the February 15, 1902 *Summit County Journal,* the Wapiti owners regularly rejoiced over "taking their lumps" in gold: "Other large nuggets—weighing eleven pounds, ninety ounces, thirty ounces, twenty-three ounces, and a number weighing over a pound each—are taken out of this and adjoining lodes of the Wapiti company's property every year."

Ten days of glory in August, 1895 provided this story in a slightly-rankled *Summit County Journal* September 11, 1895:

> *George Clavaux took out 70 ounces of coarse gold specimens and cleaned up one 36-ounce retort and one 406-ounce retort during the last ten days of August. The 512 ounces of gold represents the result of one man's labor, Mr. Clavaux, on a block of the Gold Flake lode. The Gold Flake is part of the Wapiti group. The largest nugget weighed over 2½ pounds . . . This gold, valued at $17 per ounce, or a total of $8,704, was not placed on exhibition, nor were any courtesies shown the press representatives in allowing an inspection of it, but instead, it was hustled off to the express office as if the country swarmed with bandits.*

The lucky Clavaux had a great September as well. He cleaned up 400 ounces of gold.

The gold nugget procession could trail on for pages. Leader of the nugget parade, the Wapiti Mining Company, owned more square miles of territory than any other U.S. gold mining corporation, according to the July 12, 1894 *Leadville Chronicle.* The company's prominent owner, Leadville mining man John Campion, bought the 1870s Fuller properties from an intervening owner, the Victoria Mining Company. Wapiti now owned Farncomb Hill ground and the gold coming from those claims elicited awe for its exquisite, nature-wrought, twisted-strands-of-gold beauty.

George Moon, the Wapiti company superintendent, strolled into Breckenridge on Saturday, March 8, 1897 bearing slabs of pure gold 1 ½ inches thick. This mass of solid gold, pulled as hunks from the ground, weighed in as worth $1,000. But the unrivaled beauty of the Farncomb Hill gold made its value exceed $1,000 by many times.

Almost every man, no matter what his regular occupation, also mined. Breckenridge's 2,000-strong 1890 population pursued a variety

Brilliant, energetic Ben Stanley Revett applied himself to every mining task. Phone service quit in the 1890s, so he wired his own line to connect his home, Denver Hotel, telegraph office and the Wapiti Mining Co. headquarters.

of callings, from purveyor of cigars to preacher, but most all spent time in the gulches and hills. Among them was the skiing preacher, Father John Lewis Dyer, who discovered the rich Warriors Mark Mine. He was a John Wesley-inspired circuit rider. The Wesley itinerants traveled on horseback but John Dyer used heavy 12-foot long miner's skis.

Snow Shoe Itinerant
Like the Pony Express, the Methodist circuit-riding preacher weaves a colorful strand in the fabric of Americana. John Lewis Dyer, our famous Snow Shoe Itinerant, stands as the last of these frontier preachers.

Too poor to afford transportation, Dyer in 1862 slogged on foot through deep March snow over 100 miles from Denver to first preach in Summit County's Parkville.

For the next four decades, John Lewis Dyer braved blizzards on high mountain passes and endured deprivation, hunger and poverty to serve Summit County's prospector camps. He filled the spiritual needs of a motley flock far from home and family. He preached in log mine camps, forest clearings, miners' cabins, eating houses, schoolrooms and—to his chagrin—saloons.

"The boys" in the 1860s placer mining camps around Breckenridge called him Father to express respect and endearment.

Dyer stepped into the Summit County scene at age 50. Though a tall, roughly handsome, powerful man, he was old by 1860s standards. He left Minnesota with $14.75 jangling in his pocket and the desire to see Pikes Peaks burning in his soul. Plagued by an eye ailment now thought to be simple conjunctivitis, he feared blindness and yearned to see the fabled peak before his sight failed.

After Parkville, he ministered in the towns of Breckenridge, Lincoln in French Gulch, Montezuma, Kokomo, Robinson, Dillon and Oro City (later Leadville). He visited the camps along the Swan, including Buffalo Flats, Delaware Flats, Gold Run Gulch, and Swan City. The man rose at 4 a.m. daily. His knees hit the cold dirt floor of his crude log cabin to pray before his day of Methodist ministry began.

He paused in 1880 just long enough to build the first church on the Colorado Western Slope, Father Dyer Methodist, and start the Boreas Pass town of Dyersville.

For his four decades of skiing achievement, Father Dyer earned induction to the Colorado Ski Hall of Fame in 1977. For his unfailing integrity, selflessness, service and discipline, he earned a place of honor among 16 Founders of Colorado, pioneers portrayed in stained glass in the State Capitol in Denver.

One of Father Dyer's successors failed to earn a place of honor in Breckenridge. In contrast, he was hung in effigy. The reason: he attempted to enforce the 1891 Colorado Saloon Closure Law. Breckenridge's sporting element arose as one to oppose him. Many miners religiously spent their Sabbath in the saloon. Irate revelers ended up dynamiting Passmore's stately church bell in retaliation. Too much zeal resulted in their blowing off the belfry as well.

Meanwhile the Catholics endured the decade of the 1890s with the melancholy Rev. Cornelius Alger as pastor. Father Alger, beset with money woes, low church attendance and the trials of pastoral travel across two counties, Park and Summit, moaned to his bishop, "I am convinced that my constitution will not be able to bear the strain."

Acts of Charity
By the decade's end, however, everything changed. The Catholic church

was fashionable during Breckenridge's very social late 1890s. "Two churches were in vogue at that time," the *Summit County Journal* remembered, "the Catholic Church with Rev. Father Dionysius C. Robertson as Priest and the M.E. Church (Methodist Episcopal) with Rev. Cooper as Pastor." The town loved music. Glee clubs, minstrel groups, church and community choirs, operettas and serenades raised money for worthy causes and entertained residents. Father Robertson had a beautiful voice and courtly ways. A continuous round of fairs, fetes, balls and parties allowed the popular priest to display those elegant manners. The ladies, enamored of the man, went door to door soliciting for his salary when the bishop neglected to forward the priest's check.

Fancy hats may fly off if this ladies group on horseback gallops away.

The younger ladies and girls, meanwhile, performed charity their own way. Forty or 50 little girls, supervised by teens, overflowed the home of Mrs. Sam Jones, who started Sister's Mustard Seeds, a ministry to the poor. Twice yearly, this group of girls staged an impressive entertainment at the Grand Army of the Republic Hall. All of Breckenridge's affluent bought tickets, sometimes in bunches. The money provided clothes, shoes and medical treatment for children and women in dire straights. The girls furnished a library and reading room in the Miners Hospital. They paid Denver doctors to treat boys and girls and sent a motherless crippled child to a Denver hospital for medical treatment.

Fire!

John Woods, a Methodist pastor whose 1939-published memoir supplied these details about Sister's Mustard Seeds, also recorded his role in a devastating May, 1896 fire. Breckenridge had already suffered an 1884 fire which devoured the popular Grand Central Hotel, several businesses and 15 assorted buildings on Ridge Street, doing a hefty $50,000 worth of damage to the town's 1880s commercial street. It leapt from Washington Avenue to Lincoln and from Ridge Street to Main. Now a raging blaze on upper Main Street burned buildings on both sides of the street between Washington and Adams.

Woods recalled that the able-bodied men were at work in the mines "leaving the old men, storekeepers, saloon bums and preacher to fight the flames." He helped carry out stuffed chairs and mattresses only to see them explode into fireballs when set down, due to the extreme heat generated inside the burning log buildings. Miners who saw smoke raced back to town and did what miners do best. Using their explosives, they dynamited a building to create a firebreak. The Golden, Colorado *Transcript* captured the story in May, 1896:

> *Breckenridge, Colo., May 22—Breckenridge had a narrow escape from being wiped out by fire to-day; as it was, nineteen buildings were consumed in about three hours and about sixty people were rendered homeless. The fire appears to have started in the rear of the building occupied by the family of Philip Taussig, on Main street, at the foot of Washington avenue, and was caused by the stove pipe becoming overheated . . . The fire hydrants failed to work properly, and before a good stream could be played upon the burning building it was seen that it was doomed, and the bystanders began moving the furniture and other moveables to the opposite side of the street. A strong wind blew the flames across a vacant lot, and it appeared that the business portion of the town, including the hotels, was doomed to destruction . . . The flames crossed the street and destroyed an old landmark—the Ford chop house building on the corner of Washington avenue and Main street.*

Finally, a bucket brigade taking water from a placer ditch quelled the conflagration.

While Breckenridge burrowed out many nuggets during the rich 1890s, the town also had its lumps of coal. First, the 1896 fire broke out. Then more grief followed in 1898 when two tragic murders occurred. Dr. Joseph Condon shot popular Corner Saloon owner, Johnny Dewers dead on August 4, 1898. The next week, on August 11, gangster Pug Ryan robbed the Denver Hotel game room. An attempt to capture the criminals resulted in the death of two respected citizens, Breckenridge's Ernest Conrad and Kokomo's Sumner Whitney. (For the vivid story of these incidents, see Mary Ellen Gilliland's local history, *Colorado Rascals, Scoundrels and No Goods.*) Finally, the biggest winter on record, a blockbuster that eventually buried buildings to their rooftops, stood ready to unleash its fury on Breckenridge.

Snow crowns Ten Mile peaks above Lincoln Avenue. A biker prepares to cruise down to Main Street. In winter, 1890s sledders enjoyed this hill.

The Big Snow Winter of 1898-99

Autumn lingered long that year. The first snowflakes drifted from the sky the evening of November 27, 1898. Snowfall gained momentum during the night and Breckenridge residents awoke to a full five feet of snow by 9 a.m. November 28. This was the opening number of a snowstorm extravaganza unparalleled in known Summit history. Snow poured from the skies every day from November 27 to February 20. The final tally: 32½ feet.

Breckenridge resident E.C. Peabody reported seeing no sunshine that winter—a dismal experience.

As early as December, the railway found its track blocked by snow. But the Leslie Rotary Snowplow, technological wonder of its time, managed to break through. Denver, South Park & Pacific trains tried valiantly to surmount snow-choked Boreas Pass. The trains encountered 40 to 50-foot drifts in South Park, then faced the wall of snow that inundated Boreas Pass. Seven locomotives rammed the rotary against the windpack. Right behind them, the angry Storm King Boreas blew his blustery breath, burying the freed track with huge drifts.

Finally, on February 5, 1899 after a week's lapse, a train groaned into

Breckenridge. That train was the last for 80 days. The blockade cut off Breckenridge from mail deliveries, fresh food and all other supplies until April 24, 1899.

Because the *Summit County Journal* ran out of newsprint, we have few accounts of the Big Snow Winter. Ed Auge, E.C. Peabody and Jess

Railway, renamed C&S in 1898, battled snow with rotary plow.

Oakley chronicled its events later. Jess Oakley, whose story appeared in print in 1939, volunteered to ski to Como, where trains operated, and bring back the most important letter mail. Breckenridge residents added their contributions to banker George Engle's donation and came up with about $12 for Jess—which was ample compensation. Three meals and a night's lodging cost $1 in 1899 and, as importantly, 25 cents bought the skier two whiskeys.

Oakley almost didn't live to spend his $12. When he reached the summit of Boreas Pass, more than 10 miles from Breckenridge, the skiing mailman needed shelter, a rest and a cup of hot coffee. To his dismay, he could see no sign of the town in the swirling snow. Finally, Oakley discerned a small wisp of smoke. The smoke stack from the massive one and one-half story section house lay below the 20-foot deep snow. Happily, a curl of smoke had caught Oakley's attention.

He made it safely to Como and back. However, in late February food supplies in Breckenridge reached a critical state. Around March 1, a mass town meeting was called to organize a shovel brigade to clear the 1860s wagon road. At 7 a.m. the next morning the bell at Firemen's Hall summoned a crew of more than 100 men and several horse teams to attack the prodigious snow. Ten days later with the road open, Breckenridge saw meats, fresh vegetables and even some luxuries appear on grocers' shelves.

Boreas, the 1882 railroad settlement at the Boreas Pass summit, gained its postoffice in 1896. Section house, still standing and restored, is at far right.

The Blockade Winter ended. When the first train chugged into town weeks later, everyone heard the locomotives' whistles blow. E.C. Peabody, who was a 15-year old schoolboy, remembered: "Stewart dismissed school. It was like an ant hill disturbed, two hundred school children and most of the citizens going to the depot to see the first train arrive after the blockade."

But deep snows remained in the high country through July. Tourists came on stagecoach tours to view the drifts. Sadly not until summer did searchers locate the body of Loren Waldo, a young grocery clerk who skied the pass to visit a newly-married wife in Denver. His body lay just a short distance from the Boreas section house. The section master had

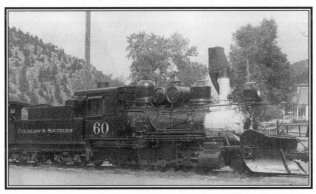

The narrow gauge, struggling to overcome alpine terrain and winter weather, served Breckenridge for 54 years 1882 to 1937, with some interruptions.

pleaded with him not to continue his ski trek alone after dark but to stay.

Winter 1898-99 stands as the only Breckenridge winter we distinguish with a capital W.

Queen Victoria died in 1901. Breckenridge reached the quintessential elegance of her Victorian era during the affluent 1890s, a moment in time never to be repeated.

PIONEER PROFILE: Edwin Carter

Edwin Carter

Visitors to Edwin Carter's 1875-built Breckenridge museum gasped in awe at the creative genius of the "Log Cabin Naturalist." Carter, a gifted taxidermist, created an elk "so life-like in strength and vitality," said guest W. R. Thomas, that you "expect it to bound away." A tiny weasel, with a sheen on her fur and a bright gleam in her eye, suckles her young in lifelike repose. A mammoth grizzly flashes fury from his glance, so accurate that you'd think the animal was breathing. It is "the largest and most complete museum of its kind in the United States, including the Smithsonian Institution," Thomas declared. The *Rocky Mountain News* on September 25, 1878 concurred, saying, it is "beyond doubt the finest collection in the state and one of the best in the country,"

Travelers keen on wildlife, along with scientists and naturalists, came from everywhere to see the specimens that Edwin Carter spent a lifetime collecting. A hunter, taxidermist and zoologist, he assembled the most remarkable collection ever gathered by an individual. Carter aimed to preserve a visual record of the abundant and varied animals and birds he found soon after his 1859 arrival in the Colorado mountains. This purpose forged like steel when he observed thousands of sportsmen arriving to decimate certain species. It hardened further when he noted two-headed bison calves and deer with mismatched antlers, a result of cyanide leaching used in mining. Carter did not miss his moment of opportunity. Among his estimated 10,000 bird and animal displays, lie studies such as his 360 mounted ptarmigans, one for almost every day of the year's subtle plumage changes.

Though trained as a taxidermist in Auburn, New York, his home state, Carter came to Colorado not to accumulate wildlife samples but to gather gold. Arriving during the Pikes Peak gold rush in 1859, he stampeded in the first wave to Russell Gulch near Blackhawk. In 1860, he joined a party bound for California Gulch at Leadville. Later he ended up in Salt Lick Gulch, above today's Silverthorne, where he combined his hunting skills with his placer mining talents. He had shot a deer with gold embedded in its teeth. He backtracked the animal to Salt Lick Creek where gold particles glittered in the sand and made the area's first placer gold strike there. He was deemed one of the finest judges of placer ground in the state of Colorado.

Carter settled for awhile at Black Hawk, where he engaged as assistant to a furrier, and increased his knowledge of taxidermy. In 1868, determined to give up prospecting for wildlife work, he came to Breckenridge. There, an observer said, "he became almost a part of the grand, inspiring wilderness which he made his haunt." He acquired a scientist's knowledge of the habits of birds and animals of the Rockies. "A conversation with Professor Carter on his favorite theme was regarded as equal to a course in text books of natural history, " said the *Fairplay Flume*, February 16, 1900.

A host who loved conversation, Edwin Carter was an amiable, fun-loving man who made lasting friendships. Many in Breckenridge counted him as a best friend, including banker George Engle. Several boys bore his name, including Edwin Carter Kaiser, son of the local butcher, and Carter Yust, son of the Blue River rancher.

His sense of humor evidenced in the mounted owl named "Boss Tweed" because it so closely resembled Nast's caricatures of that New York gang boss. A stuffed bear, "bearing" a wine glass in one paw and a wine bottle in the other amused visitors.

During his 1880s museum visit, W.R. Thomas left us rare insight into Carter's personality. He wrote,

A knock at the cabin door is answered by a tall, spare man, about sixty years of age, with gray hair and beard, a clear full eye, and a genial countenance. He gives you a cordial welcome, and beneath his somewhat careless garb you readily discern the manners of a born gentleman and the instincts of a student. Chatting pleasantly with this pioneer resident of the mountains, you learn that he is a native of New York Sate, that he was raised in the dry goods business, that he learned the art of taxidermy in Auburn, N.Y. from a Scotch Highlander who had been a game keeper in the old country, that he drifted west, and was in business in Council Bluffs, Iowa, when he joined the great army of gold hunters, which sought Colorado in 1859. In . . . Breckenridge in 1870 (he) began to accumulate specimens for his museum, having conceived the idea of making a complete collection of the fauna of Colorado.

Though he sold duplicate specimens to make a living, Carter refused to part with any key item in his menagerie. He turned down better offers to finally transfer his collection to launch the Denver Museum of Natural History, which built its first building to house an initial 3,000 Carter specimens. While negotiations dragged on, Edwin Carter sickened and died, a victim of arsenic poisoning, the chemical he used to create and preserve his world-famous wildlife collection.

Carter's body lay in state in the Colorado State Capitol in recognition of his contribution to state and nation—an honor rarely granted to an ordinary citizen.

District Courts building (l. center) would soon yield to new brick courthouse.

8

The 1900s

Breckenridge celebrated its 50th year, 1909, with a binge—of progress. This chapter will highlight that year's achievements. First, a stately brick courthouse, its cornerstone laid July 31, 1909, marked the old camp's transition from a half-log settlement, half-Victorian town to a mature mine community. Second, the Reiling dredge, launched in 1909, signaled a shift from lode mining's lead in the gold profit picture to a new era of dredge gold dominance. The gold gobbling dredge boats, a highly-effective mode of placer mining, changed everyday people's jobs and lives. And third, these same gold boats tripled Breckenridge's mining output from previous years to make 1909 a flush mining year.

Like the dredge boat, which swung around in its pond on a spud driven into the riverbed, Breckenridge pivoted during the 1900s to face its future. The decade of the 1900s proved to be the last period of idealistic bliss, of capitalist pride, of unflawed faith in the goodness of life.

Happy 1900s couples enjoy era of bliss.

The town would undergo the tragedy of World War I and the loss of local boys to the war in Europe. Breckenridge would never again enjoy the spread of benefits from mining across the community. Instead, dredge companies, which employed only a few workers, would take the profits. The Gold Pan Shops, new in Breckenridge's 1900s, provided jobs for machinists but not many for miners. The town's 50th signaled change.

A naïve Breckenridge celebrated its jubilee with festivities to mark laying the cornerstone of the new courthouse. The $43,000 courthouse, located at 208 Lincoln Avenue, features Colonial-Revival architecture, a magnificent four-sided white cupola and entry pediments painted with mining and rail-road scenes. Visitors can see them today, for the Summit County courthouse still serves citizens from its original brick structure. A parade of 75 Masons in full regalia marched to a brass band. A chorus of 50 local vocalists raised a joyous anthem as the Masons set the granite corner-stone in place. Ladies in dainty white dresses and big hats, gents in three-piece suits and derby hats gathered that Saturday, July 31, 1909 to witness the grand event.

A stately 1909 Summit County courthouse stamped Breckenridge as mature.

Breckenridge rose to its moment. Times were good. Residents returned to their homes after the celebration to switch on electric lights at dusk, ring up friends on the telephone and watch in admiration as a motorcar hurtled at breakneck speed (limit: 10 mph) down Main Street.

Those shiny horseless carriages cost a hefty $3,700 for an American-built auto until Henry Ford introduced his economical Model T in 1908. At $850—windshield, tops and headlamps cost extra—the Model T caught on big. Its high axles and 3.5-inch wide tires straddled roads rutted by wagon wheels. But high mountain pass travel choked the early engines, causing vapor lock, and the lack of plowed roads put autos up on blocks for the winter. Despite these drawbacks, autos created the aura of wealth and power—just what Breckenridge's mineral magnates craved.

Mining moguls like Ben Stanley Revett, Captain Lemuel Kingsbury and George Evans had swaggered onto the mining stage, flashing diamond stick-pins and gold nugget watch chains. Now they traveled in the town's first automobiles. George Evans navigated Breckenridge roadways in a Stanley Steamer and motored home to a plush residence complete with its own thea-ter and a pet monkey.

Mining, the industry that financed all that swagger, had undergone major changes. New mining equipment— oil drills for deep ground testing and churn drills for deep digging, Ingersoll power drills for opening mine tunnels, along with concentrating tables for shaking more gold from milled ore— all caused a resurgence from late 1890s doldrums. In addition, the Wilfley Table, invented in 1895 by Arthur C. Wilfley in the Ten Mile Canyon town of Kokomo, jump-started mining's progress. It allowed ore mills to get more gold out of the ore.

Despite these advances, the year 1909 saw only four lode mines ship-ping steadily. According to geologist Leslie Ransome, they were French Gulch's Wellington and Country Boy, Australia Gulch's Sally Barber and Illinois Gulch's Laurium, also called Blue Flag.

The Reiling Dredge

The biggest change, however, occurred not in hardrock mining but in Breckenridge's strongest suit, placer mining. The gold boats churned through glacially-laid river gravels to expose and collect bedrock de-posits. Breckenridge boosted its placer gold production from about $10,000 a year through the 1890s, according to Charles Henderson, to $145,370 in 1908 when dredges began to make an impact. But the next year, 1909, when the Reiling dredge came on board, production jumped to a staggering $405,360. This amount, which represents placer gold only, was big money in 1909. The dredge companies exulted.

Daily Life

Less of this money ended up in the pockets of citizens. But they managed to enjoy mountain life without diamond pins and auto cars. Many of them rode bicycles, all the rage, to a bounty of recreation events enjoyed in 1900s Breckenridge. The fat-tire Montrose bikes, like today's mountain bike, provided stability for mountain-road riders. The price: $16.50 at Finding's Hardware.

Sports-minded Breckenridge took up bicycling, the new rage across America.

Baseball enjoyed enthusiastic support, and competition with other local towns ran hot. A Breckenridge ladies basketball team now played at Fireman's Hall. Foot races, parades, hardrock drilling contests, anvil ringing competitions and horse races took place on Main Street, built wide to accommodate turning wagon trains.

People didn't regard walking as a sport. But John McElroy, the champion walker of Summit County, amazed locals by walking to Alma before breakfast. McElroy's fast pace and long stride turned heads. His comrade, Paul Hanniwald, who lived in Leadville, traveled to Breckenridge to play in the orchestra for the town's elegant dances. Impatient at the engine's pace over Fremont Pass, he jumped off to walk to town. He beat the train.

Despite the stamina of these men, Breckenridge and Americans in general enjoyed an average life expectancy of only 37 years. Most died of pneumonia, influenza, tuberculosis, diarrhea or heart disease and stroke. (After years of struggle, Breckenridge got a first-rate hospital building in 1906.) Only 14 percent of Americans had a bathtub. Only six percent had graduated from high school.

That number stood ready to rise in 1908 Breckenridge, for the new brick schoolhouse built at Lincoln Avenue and Harris Street provided youth their first opportunity for a full high school diploma. Pupils had been able to complete tenth grade only. Students came from all over the county, many spending the school term in Breckenridge, due to travel distances. The new school also relieved crowding in the old 1882 schoolhouse where 187 students crammed into a building designed for a maximum of 150.

1908 schoolhouse boosted civic pride. Pupils could now complete 12th grade.

A few of these youths came from "down the Blue," where homesteaders had taken up ranches on the pastoral grasslands north of Silverthorne. When plentiful jobs for miners dried up, Breckenridge residents looked to ranching for a living. Tired of the hazards of mining, such as silicosis lung disease caused by rock dust and injury from grisly accidents, they began an exodus from town life to a primitive rural existence. The 1862 U.S. homestead law had allowed ranchers who worked the land and fulfilled regulations to gain ownership of 160 acres. In the early 1900s, miners and their families moved in increasing numbers to the ranchlands. By 1910, families on the Blue numbered 150.

First to go north, as early as the 1880s, were Edward Charles Yust, a partner with Luther Smart in a Breckenridge saloon; Peter Engle, partner with his brother, George, first in a saloon then in the Engle Brothers

Exchange Bank; and the British-born Pharo family, also Breckenridge business owners. They homesteaded at remote Colorow, located along today's Gore Pass Road near Kremmling. Direct descendant Jim Yust still lives on the 1884-established Yust Ranch. Though they lived amid awesome scenery below beautiful Eagles Nest peak, these families faced isolation, loneliness and lack. But they stuck it out.

Farncomb Hill gold beautified the bride's ring when Clara Yust (front row, in white) married Wynn Howe (l. of Clara) in 1905. Big Yust family turned out.

Swandyke, An Alpine Camp

Another spot equally-remote, hummed with mining activity: the new town of Swandyke perched just below the Continental Divide on the middle fork of the Swan River. Although occupied through the 1890s with come-and-go prospectors, Swandyke emerged as a real town by 1898 and now housed a hotel, saloon, butcher and barber shops, livery stable, sawmill, plus two stores— one in town and one in nearby Bull Gulch. Stagecoach service transported visitors to the town, some a bit shaken after the hairy descent from the pass. A massive snowslide during the blockbuster winter of 1898-99 had destroyed Swandyke's only ore mill, sweeping away valuable ore with it. The town moved ahead in the 1900s with its Carrie, Pompeii, Brilent, Three Kings and Isabella mines. However, by 1910 excitement waned, population plummeted and the Swandyke postoffice closed its doors.

Mining Accidents

Life wasn't all roses back in Breckenridge. Despite the blithe optimism of the 1900s, tragedy occurred. At the Puzzle Mine in 1902, a cave-in pinned Breckenridge postmaster and miner William Stouffer in a small sea of fallen boulders and rock. Men poured out of Breckenridge to help save Stouffer, working from 10 a.m. till 8 p.m. without success. Secondary avalanches of loose rock threatened to strike the rescuers. Due to tight quarters, no tools could be used. Instead the men clawed the rock with bare hands. Slides re-buried the victim several times despite the heroic efforts of workers. Finally they exposed the trapped Stouffer to discover his leg buried by a boulder. When workers gave up hope, Dr. J. F. Condon arrived to urge, "Let's give it one more try." They did, and freed the mangled miner. Condon had to amputate the leg on the scene to save Stouffer's life.

A different but no less deadly threat faced dredge workers. In 1905, Ben Stanley Revett's Reliance Gold Dredging Company had constructed a double-lift gold boat of his own design—Breckenridge's first successful gold dredge. In summer 1909 workers overhauled Revett's steam-driven Reliance and adapted it for a new and little-known energy, electricity. This advance began a series of electrocutions on Breckenridge gold dredges caused by ignorance of electricity, especially when combined with water. The town gathered at Valley Brook Cemetery to mourn a 24-year old with a young wife, killed by electrocution on an early dredge.

The dredges worked on ponds of their own creation as they scooped out gold-bearing gravel from the dredge front and deposited the tailings behind, creating a basin on the waterway. Not only electrocutions but also drownings endangered dredge workers.

That same buried treasure sought by dredges drove George Evans and his Gold Pan Mining Company to excavate the 90-foot deep Gold Pan Pit in South Breckenridge in 1901-02. This massively-expensive and minimally-productive effort was accomplished using Evans' own invention, the Evans Hydraulic Elevator. The goal: to mine the rich bedrock in the Maggie Pit with its promise of delivering many years of wealth. The outcome: not much. George Evans left town and his 90-foot gold pit is now the Maggie Pond, a scenic lake below Peak 9.

A noted achievement accompanied the Gold Pan venture. The Gold

Pan Shops, reputedly the finest machine shops west of the Mississippi, emerged when the Gold Pan Company realized the extent of its need for machinery and equipment. So the company built its first-rate machine shops near south Ridge Street and produced machinery of every kind, plus its own electricity.

Railway Shutdown

In 1907, the old Denver, South Park & Pacific narrow gauge, now called the Colorado & Southern, ceased operation due to a trainmen's strike. For weeks, business ground to a halt. Not a single freight car moved. Ore shipments stopped. The railroad lost $100 a day in ore freight from the big Wellington Mine alone. Provisions arriving by horseback or wagon brought high prices.

1907 strike halted trains. Engine 9, above, will return to Breckenridge.

This began a rail service controversy which would continue over years, culminating in the shutdown of the C&S in 1937. During times when profits from ore freight dipped, the railroad didn't want to continue rail service to Breckenridge. People received no mail, their only significant means of outside contact. Locals demanded that their railway lifeline continue.

The C&S resumed service. Breckenridge's 1900s drew to a close without its residents recognizing that an era had ended. Fifty-year old Breckenridge witnessed the demise of the individual prospector. He had prospered there for a half century, ever since the summer 1859 arrivals and their standard-bearer, Ruben J. Spaulding, cried "Eureka!"

PIONEER PROFILE: Robert W. Foote

After Robert W. Foote came to Breckenridge in February, 1880, no one else could match his warm-hearted consideration of the needs of his neighbors.

Foote owned the popular Denver Hotel, Breckenridge's number one stopping place. Guests of distinction mingled in the hotel dining room with prospectors Bob had taken under his hospitable wing. He fed those down on their luck, sometimes for months at a time, according to his nephew, Ed Auge, and never saw a need he failed to meet.

During the Blockade Winter of 1898-99, when trains stopped bringing provisions to a snowbound Breckenridge, Bob Foote himself needed a favor. His little daughter, Ella, refused to eat because she had no butter. Bob visited Mrs. Almeda Peabody who ran the Colorado House. When he asked for butter, despite its scarcity and her need to put it on her boardinghouse table, Mrs. Peabody gave in. But only because Bob Foote asked.

People called him "Lucky Bob Foote" because every rock he touched turned to gold—or lead, or zinc, as in the case of his famous Wellington Mine. His gold finds, regarded with awe by townsfolk, number too many to detail here. A short list appears below.

Bonanza strike: Strapped by his purchase of the Denver Hotel, Foote found himself in a cash flow crisis in operating the establishment. He needed money. He asked a Frenchman, George Clavaux, to take a grubstake from him and go tap into an area of the Gold Flake tunnel, part of a large Farncomb Hill mine. Foote's friend, Ed White, had always had a hunch the rock there would produce. Days went by and the anxious hotel proprietor heard nothing. With creditors closing in, Clavaux showed up in Breckenridge, his gold pouch bulging with nuggets and a mile-wide grin across his face.

390 ounces of gold in one week: Foote and George Clavaux later leased the Gold Flake. In early October, 1896 they took out 390 ounces of gold, including a choice 19-ounce nugget. This single weekly cleanup brought the output of their lease to more than 1,500 ounces of gold in less than two months.

Nugget suspended by a golden strand: With his brother-in-law, Peter Cummings, Foote took a lease on Farncomb Hill's Boss Mine. A sharp cry from Cummings brought Foote to his partner's side, fearing injury. Instead Cummings raised his candle to illuminate a large gold nugget hanging by a thread. Behind it lay a stunning pocket of gold nuggets.

Robert W. Foote owned, leased or operated many mines around Breckenridge. He located French Gulch's rich Minnie Mine with A. M. Rich and John Mairs soon after he arrived in Breckenridge at age 19, according to the *Summit County Journal.* Other mines, the Cincinnati; the Ella, and Oro, neighbors on Mineral Hill; the Brooks-Snyder on Shock Hill; the Boss on Farncomb Hill; the Germania on Little Mountain; the Mountain Pride on Bald Mountain all poured gold into Bob Foote's waiting pockets.

His biggest achievement, however, lay in the Wellington Mine, Breckenridge's most famous. In 26 years of operation it produced nearly $20 million and paid its stockholders about $2 million during World War I alone.

How he got the Wellington is an interesting story. As a newcomer, a young Bob had arrived with $30 in his pocket. Nevertheless, his generosity came into play when Uncle Johnny Mairs, a mining veteran, needed help. The old prospector never forgot the youth's kindness. Years later, he let Foote in on the Wellington when the incredibly-rich mine was only a prospect. In January, 1903, that prospect became a reality with a notable strike. The Wellington produced zinc, lead, gold and silver. Its owners, a local group of prominent businessmen including Bob Foote, then purchased the Oro Mine, with its 100-man workforce, in 1906. Foote, the mine's first general manager, oversaw the mine during peak development years, leaving his post in 1910. (For a detailed history of Breckenridge's best mine ever, see Ed Auge's *History of the Breckenridge Mining District 1859-1937* by Marion Street Publishing.)

Brilliance and luck motivated Bob Foote to put his energy into mining. But he also poured himself into community service. He held posts as Breckenridge mayor, school district president, Democratic party chairman, Breckenridge baseball team manager and more.

Foote, a staunch member of a leading men's club, the Warm Stove Mine, supported fellow member, Dr. Joseph Condon, accused in the 1898 shooting death of the unarmed Johnny Dewers.

Condon admitted pumping three bullets into Dewers in a dispute over attention to Dewers' wife but he pleaded self-defense. Bob Foote raised the $10,000 cash for the doctor's bail and testified on Condon's behalf, as did other prominent Breckenridge gents.

Foote had a long and happy marriage to Margaret Burnheimer, the local belle he wed on February 26, 1888. The couple had one daughter, Ella, who grew up to marry mining expert and newspaper editor, J. A. Theobald. Direct Theobald descendants live around Breckenridge today.

Born in L'Anse, Michigan June 26, 1860, Robert W. Foote died on January 11, 1923 after three years of suffering from his final illness. His grave is in Valley Brook Cemetery. The *Summit County Journal* on January 20, 1923 recalled:

He had never seen anyone want for a necessity and his principal aim in life was to cheer up the down-hearted . . . His was the spirit that made towns and men.

Robert Foote's Denver Hotel anchored Main Street's west side. Man beside apron-wearing bartender is probably Foote. Upstairs: Mrs. Foote and Ella.

The Wellington Mine, Breckenridge's outstanding long-time producer, yielded lead, zinc, gold and silver (in that quantitative order). It grouped several mines, including the historic Oro, and, with that, spanned many decades from the 1880s, finally closing for good in 1973. Robert Foote's well-known friends, Journal editor O.K. Gaymon, Gold Pan Mining Company manager George H. Evans and attorney J.T. Hogan joined Foote as investors in the 1901-formed Colorado and Wyoming Development Company which owned the mine in the 1900s.

9

The 1910s

County Sheriff Walter Thomas (upper r.) served with the Red Cross in WWI.

A mine cave-in happens suddenly, often with no warning. World War I, 1914-1918, crashed in on the American consciousness just that suddenly. In Breckenridge, the war shattered turn of the century idealism and yanked boys from their homes. A second and more deadly rockfall let loose when the worldwide Spanish influenza epidemic crippled the town and ended the lives of many local men, women and children.

A less serious crusher came with Prohibition. It became law on January 1, 1916. Breckenridge's saloons, long a bastion of male retreat and a comfortable haven from the pressures of job and household, closed their swinging doors.

While men faced the fact that the brass rail and foaming stein no longer hallowed their hours of freedom, women celebrated new liberties. They shed the constriction of their whalebone corsets. Some began to bob their hair, a freedom to continue in the 1920s despite censure from preachers and consternation from fathers and husbands.

In their turn, men plunged into the new sport of ski jumping, introduced to Summit County by Norwegian jumper Peter Prestrud. He built a ski jump at Frisco's Excelsior Mine, then turned his considerable skills to a state-of-the-art jump on Lake Hill above Old Dillon. This legendary achievement drew competitors from around the U.S. and the world. (Prestrud earned admission to the Colorado Ski Hall of Fame because of it.) Breckenridge entered the ski scene with gusto, building its own ski jump in 1919. Located near the Pence-Miller Ditch, the Shock Hill Ski Course had a ten-foot wide, 90-foot long trestle-supported jump.

World War I

When the U.S. entered the European conflict in 1917, Breckenridge greeted the occasion with songs, cheers, bells and patriotic speeches. The message: produce more, use less, promote the war effort and be a patriot. Breckenridge high school students promoted purchasing war savings stamps in 1918. By year's end, they brought Breckenridge to

German U-boat attacks on U.S. merchant ships caused isolationist America to enter World War I on April 6, 1917 under Woodrow Wilson (in top hat).

nearly the top of the nation for per capita savings stamp sales. Men signed up for the draft. Women, including Margaret Foote, met at Red Cross headquarters to knit and sew warm clothes for children freezing in war-torn countries.

This burst of enthusiasm met grim reality when Breckenridge relinquished 56 of its best and finest young men to the European front. A roster of Colorado soldiers, 1917-1918, published by the Colorado National Guard lists well-known local names such as Charles E. Condon, Walter Dodge, Charles Fletcher, William H. Forman, Melvin Gaymon, Robert Gore, Edmund Leuthold, Clyde McAdoo, and John and Joseph McGee among the 56 who recorded their address as Breckenridge.

Walter Thomas, Summit County sheriff from 1913-15, wrote regular reports from the front, published by the *Summit County Journal*. He worked with the Rocky Mountain Division of the American Red Cross as a lieutenant in England, Turkey and Greece.

Influenza

If the war weren't enough, influenza took so many family members, loved ones and friends that Breckenridge and all of Summit County staggered from its onslaught. The *Journal* stopped publishing news. Instead its front page carried only obituaries. John Wood, a former Father Dyer Methodist Church pastor, lost his wife in childbirth then saw his baby daughter succumb to influenza. A trained nurse for the infant had the flu and infected the baby. A grieving Wood wrote:

> *Upon my return from Denver after daughter's funeral, I found the town of Breckenridge literally full of influenza. All public gatherings were closed. Dr. E. Vance Graham was going night and day . . . Then the doctor was taken down. His wife, asthmatic, had already been taken and it had developed into double pneumonia.*

Breckenridge closed its schools, churches and theater to control the rampant advance of the killer disease. When cases diminished, relieved residents rode the train to Denver for the annual National Western Stock Show. Tragically, Denver media suppressed news of widespread recurrence of influenza there. Those who attended the Stock Show from Breckenridge and other Colorado towns came back sick and re-introduced influenza in another big wave of sickness and death. Twenty-five new cases were reported by Friday after the Stock Show. Many influenza victims succumbed not to flu but to the pneumonia that set in after the initial disease.

Prohibition

Like most Western towns, Breckenridge began its life as a town with a handful of buildings, including a watering hole called the Pioneer Saloon. The early saloon served as a community hall, voting place, venue for the Miners Court, meeting house for gospel preaching and a social haven for a mostly-male society. The saloon as an American institution sometimes took on a raucous bent but its role as a community center prevailed.

Prohibition abolished the saloon and all its close-held traditions. After New Years Day, 1916, moonshiners operated stills in abandoned mine tunnels and isolated gulches, brewing white lightnin'. Bootleggers, the distribution arm of the business, sold the high-proof whiskey to places like Bradley's Saloon, (today's Gold Pan on Main Street) where a back room bar and gambling den hummed behind locked doors. (See Gilliland's *Colorado Rascals, Scoundrels and No Goods* for full coverage of Prohibition.)

Tiger

The ban on booze lasted till 1933. The life-span of Prohibition roughly matched the boom-bust cycle of Tiger, a new town born in 1917 and located in the nearby Swan River Valley. Prospectors Willey, Reed and Smith had discovered the Tiger Lode as early as 1864, and neighboring mines such as the bonanza-rich IXL, with its Swallow, Royal Tiger, Highland Mary and Eureka claims produced good quality ore through the 1880s and 90s. However, the whole group, along with its five-acre mill site, sold for back taxes in 1912, after a ruinous cave in at the IXL. Thomas A. Brown, for whom Brown's Gulch is named, snapped up the properties. Brown's colleague, John A. Traylor, later acquired Brown's rich mining ground to advance his modest personal dream: he wanted to build "the biggest mining empire in the world." With that dream came the town of Tiger.

By 1917 Traylor had discovered untapped potential in the then-abandoned IXL lode. The property, assessed for only $780 in 1910, blossomed with a new 500-ton ore mill and a tunnel connection to the rich Cashier Mine. On May 17, 1917 Traylor organized the Royal Tiger Mines Company. Traylor also established his benevolent company mine town called Tiger. After just one year the new town buzzed with a 15,000-foot daily capacity sawmill, a 16-room boardinghouse, a school and a growing number of residents. Population reached 75 families by 1919, the year the town postoffice opened. Now 40 buildings, a store (which sold food and supplies to residents at cost), hospital, office, rooming house, cottages and cabins comprised a real town. In a few more years, the town would add a fine school and public library.

The rise of Tiger gave employment to both men and women from Breckenridge. While men worked in the mines, mill or sawmill, women

Men Wanted at

TIGER

**AN IDEAL PLACE FOR MEN
WHO WANT TO WORK**

Room for eight more families

Living conditions the best
that can be offered anywhere

Eight more single men wanted

THE TIGER SCHOOL

is of the highest grade, founded on the idea that

EDUCATION
Is The Hope of The Future

Be a Tiger

ran the boardinghouse or taught school. Teenage girls served meals and sorted ore. In every case, families were favored. Married fathers earned more money than single men in Tiger.

Tiger gave a boost to Breckenridge because sporadic service from the Colorado & Southern had threatened town jobs. The old Denver, South Park & Pacific Railroad had gone into receivership in 1898 and emerged anew as the C&S. In May 1911, the Chamber of Commerce still petitioned the railway to resume running trains. A lawsuit finally settled the issue. The man who led the lawsuit to its happy conclusion was a decades-long Breckenridge citizen and leader.

William Harrison Briggle

A Chamber of Commerce executive, Briggle worked untiringly to help win the railroad case, according to a later September 27, 1924 *Summit County Journal* article. The lawsuit forced the C&S to keep the narrow gauge link to the outside world open. A vital connection, the railway served as Breckenridge's lifeline. William Briggle's energy didn't stop with the lawsuit. As cashier at his brother-in-law George Engle's bank, he worked a full week. But he also managed to serve Breckenridge in the following roles:

> Mayor, Town of Breckenridge,
> Member, Breckenridge Town Board (several times),
> Director, Metal Mining Association,
> Head, World War I Red Cross Chapter (with honors),
> Member, Board of County Commissioners,
> Volunteer, Blue River Hose Company,
> Genial Host, Briggle House social events.

Born in Stark County, Ohio in 1861, Briggle came to Breckenridge with his parents November 4, 1886 at age 15. He first engaged in a book and stationery business, then joined the bank in 1892. He married the sociable Miss Kathleen Trotter and the pair began three decades of hospitality, hosting dinners, parties and socials in their Romanesque Revival home at 104 North Harris Street. The Briggle House, now open as a Breckenridge Heritage Alliance museum, stands as a marker to an hourglass of time, now run out, of Breckenridge social elegance.

The William Briggles hosted parties in their home, now a historical museum.

Mining in the 1910s

The capital that floated the town's social ship of state came from stream bedrock, gold-rich gulches and hardrock mineral hoards surrounding the town. But mining in the decade of the 1910s was emblazoned by one shining star, the Wellington Mine. At times the Wellington outperformed even the lucrative gold dredges in dollar output. In 1911, the Wellington paid stockholders two dividends of $50,000 each. By 1920, total dividends paid would exceed $2.5 million, according to Bill Fountain's unpublished "Wellington Mine History."

Meanwhile the Reiling dredge continued to gouge gold from river beds. In 1914, for example, after two $15,000 and $16,000 weekly cleanups in June, the gold boat averaged a sweet $1,000 per day for the rest of the year.

Gold's best year during the 1910s decade, according to Charles W. Henderson, was 1915 with its weighty $680,144 output. For a decade that tumbled a rockslide of troubles on Breckenridge, this banner year stood at the highest over a 40-year span, a bright spot in a turbulent decade.

PIONEER PROFILE: Johann Christian Kaiser

Johann Christian Kaiser

Christ Kaiser, Breckenridge's German grocer, stands silhouetted against history as rock solid as the granite Peak 8 he viewed from his Lincoln Avenue store front. A reserved, matter-of-fact, business-like man, according to his great-granddaughter Roxie Kaiser Knudsen, he possessed a heart of gold. From that generous heart he contributed to his community for over 50 years. Using supplies from his grocery store, he grubstaked prospectors down on their luck, gave away groceries to the needy, provided cash to poor families, used his market's delivery wagon to haul furniture, equipment or supplies for neighbors and offered encouragement to all who needed a lift. "He struggled with his store," remarked Roxie Kaiser Knudson, "because he gave everything away."

This steady butcher, born in Michelfield, Winterburg, Germany in 1856, came to America at a young age. Kaiser landed in Breckenridge in 1878, just as the lode mining boom ignited and population skyrocketed. A patriot, the 22-year old sought U.S.

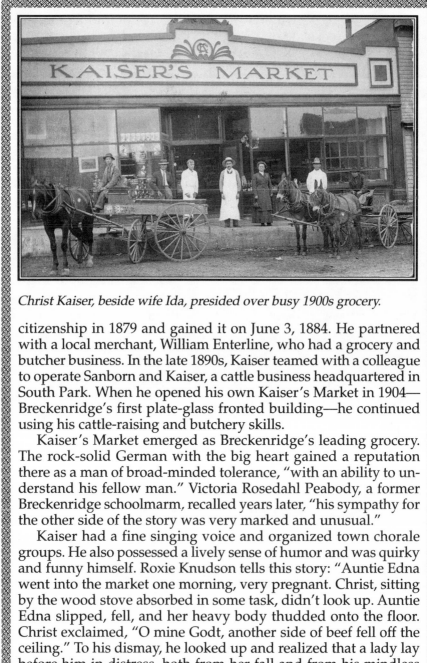

Christ Kaiser, beside wife Ida, presided over busy 1900s grocery.

citizenship in 1879 and gained it on June 3, 1884. He partnered with a local merchant, William Enterline, who had a grocery and butcher business. In the late 1890s, Kaiser teamed with a colleague to operate Sanborn and Kaiser, a cattle business headquartered in South Park. When he opened his own Kaiser's Market in 1904—Breckenridge's first plate-glass fronted building—he continued using his cattle-raising and butchery skills.

Kaiser's Market emerged as Breckenridge's leading grocery. The rock-solid German with the big heart gained a reputation there as a man of broad-minded tolerance, "with an ability to understand his fellow man." Victoria Rosedahl Peabody, a former Breckenridge schoolmarm, recalled years later, "his sympathy for the other side of the story was very marked and unusual."

Kaiser had a fine singing voice and organized town chorale groups. He also possessed a lively sense of humor and was quirky and funny himself. Roxie Knudson tells this story: "Auntie Edna went into the market one morning, very pregnant. Christ, sitting by the wood stove absorbed in some task, didn't look up. Auntie Edna slipped, fell, and her heavy body thudded onto the floor. Christ exclaimed, "O mine Godt, another side of beef fell off the ceiling." To his dismay, he looked up and realized that a lady lay before him in distress, both from her fall and from his mindless comment. Though angry, she was unhurt.

Christ dove into community life in Breckenridge from his arrival through the next 50 years. He married Swedish immigrant Ida Charlotte Sandell on November 4, 1886. The popular couple had three sons, Edwin Carter (named for the naturalist) in 1888; Harold Robert less than a year later in 1889; and Carl Albert in 1891. Irene May, a baby daughter born in 1893, died of pneumonia at only nine months. Christ and Ida raised not just their three boys, but also Ida's sister's girl, Hannah, and two nephews from Germany, Emile and Otto Wurst.

Christ Kaiser served as Breckenridge mayor and also did several stints on the town board. A loyal Democrat, he became a delegate to a National Democratic Convention. A charter member of the local Masonic Lodge, he continued through its 50th anniversary in 1931. Like most Breckenridge businessmen, he engaged in various mining ventures including the Morning Star Mine. For years he held posts on the local school board and helped oversee the design and construction of the new Breckenridge school in 1908. Kaiser was elected county commissioner for three terms.

During the Big Snow Winter of 1898-99 the railroad, blockaded by snow, cut off supplies to Kaiser's store. Christ resorted to questionable methods to acquire the beef he needed. He appropriated his wife's precious milk cow. Ida's pet ended up as "pur-loined" steaks and roasts in Kaiser's Market.

Mrs. Kaiser refused to risk having another cow. Instead she got a goat for milk and kept it under her eye, tied up to the side of the house. Children on their way to school pestered the goat and made it mean. One day as Ida bent over her laundry basket to hang wash on the line, the goat butted her full force in the backside. The proper Breckenridge matron, petticoats displayed, rolled head over heels two or three times. The next day goat meat was on sale at Kaiser's Market.

Near the end of Kaiser's life, his son, Edwin, returned to Breckenridge to run the grocery for his ailing father. Johann Christian Kaiser died on October 3, 1932. His grieved life partner, Ida, followed him in death just six weeks later.

In a newspaper tribute to Kaiser, Victoria Rosedahl Peabody wrote,

Very few men in a generation can secure and hold the high esteem in a community as did Christian Kaiser . . . The force of

personality possessed by Christ Kaiser, as he was lovingly called, has been felt by many.

Most notable townsfolk had one obituary. Christ Kaiser's three memorials, full of accolades, remain as a rock-solid monument to his standing in Breckenridge.

Kaiser's boys, Edwin, Harold and Carl, ride tricycles in matching suits. The historic home, with later additions, is now a restaurant at 130 S. Ridge.

10

The 1920s

L ost hope characterized Breckenridge in the 1920s. Many refused to admit that, except for river dredging, the once-rich mining ground had exhausted its yield. Breckenridge lost its dominance to the rising-star town of Tiger.

And the town faced a new humiliation: the Tonopah Placers Company's gold dredge demolished the town's main access road, ripped out trees and crushed or relocated buildings on a relentless push to mine the Blue River right through town.

Yet tenacious individuals clung to their conviction that fortunes in gold still lay waiting. John A. Traylor, who aspired to create a 1920s mining empire, personifies the dashed dreams of the 1920s. So does an intriguing story found buried in the manuscript collection of the Denver Public Library. Volunteers cleaning out the Gaymon House, home of an early *Summit County Journal* editor, found the dusty papers which ended up in the library. Their tale captures the delusion of mining in the 1920s.

A few refused to quit.

The Legend of the Lost Dutchman

The story begins back in 1881, Summit County's biggest gold year ever. A crusty newcomer loaded a pack train of six burros in Breckenridge while an old prospector watched. The stranger hoisted a cookstove on one burro, sacks, boxes and cartons of groceries on another. One burro bore picks, shovels and gold pans. Another wobbled under an unusual trunk of galvanized iron.

"Where are you headed?" called the old prospector. "None of your

Miner's pack train.

damn business," came the reply, laced with a Dutch accent. Curious, the old prospector trailed the Dutchman out of town. Finally the stranger turned, fixed his rifle on the old man and yelled "You old fool, go back to town unless you want someone to carry you back." The prospector gave up but noticed when the Dutchman returned to Breckenridge in late September. The stranger confided to a stable worker, "I'm going to Denver for the winter and I'll have me the biggest schooner of beer that gold dust can buy. I've been drinking water for so long that my stomach is kicking."

The Dutchman reappeared in Breckenridge in April and repeated the burro train scene, returning again in the fall. This happened for several years until one winter a Breckenridge miner met the Dutchman in a Denver saloon at 15th and Larimer. He watched wide-eyed as the Dutchman poured gold dust from a leather bag onto the bartender's troy-weight scales. The Dutchman received a generous handful of gold coins in change. The Breckenridge miner struck up a conversation with the Dutchman, who after many beers boasted that he "had the world by the tail." However, he refused to reveal the location of his rich Breckenridge placer ground.

His summers in the hills continued till 1887. Then the Dutchman "took a bullet in the breast" during a Denver barroom scrap and carried his mine secret to the grave.

Andrew Kilstrup, the man who learned of this legend "from a fine Christian gentleman," determined in the mid-1920s to search for the Lost Dutchman Mine. His enthusiasm persuaded a group of Denver investors to bankroll his search. These prominent businessmen, who owned the National Savings Syndicate, joined with mining engineer Horace Walters to underwrite Kilstrup's quest.

After three years of frustration, Kilstrup on July 2, 1928 telegraphed an exultant message: "Found Lost Dutchman. Come at once." He followed with a letter the next day: "I feel like a millionaire!" In fact, the joyous prospector sent his distinguished backers two letters that same day, each gloating over his find. "Just think of it, dear pals, we have 160 acres of the best gold placer ground in the state of Colorado!" He reported finding two garnets shining in his gold pan, along with platinum and two, three and four colors to the pan. He revealed his location as just below the Pence-Miller Ditch.

This photo accompanied The Lost Dutchman papers.

Engineer Horace Walter's report on July 27, 1928 skimmed some froth off Kilstrup's enthusiasm. The garnets were only red crystals. The gold that flashed in the pan needed considerable re-evaluation by testing. The platinum may have been a myth. Indeed, the Lost Dutchman Mine proved itself a bubble inflated by the fervor of one man, Andrew Kilstrup, who still believed in Breckenridge gold.

His hand-written letters remain in the Denver library, as does his location certificate and a typed rendition of the Lost Dutchman tale. Did Kilstrup concoct the legend? He needed backers to finance his fantasy of a return to a bountiful era now gone. Maybe he still believed.

Royal Tiger Mines

Another visionary required funds to finance his ambition, this time on a vastly-larger scale than Kilstrup's dream. John A. Traylor envisioned a mining empire in today's Golden Horseshoe (east up the gold-seamed Swan Valley, around the glittering Parkville-Farncomb Hill arch and west down gold-riddled French Gulch). His grandiose goal: to steer the helm of the world's largest mining conglomerate, the Royal Tiger Mines Company. Traylor had the ego to drive him to success. He possessed the charisma to persuade investors to part with the necessary cash.

His company town of Tiger became the shining jewel of Colorado mine towns. Early town progress covered in the previous chapter advanced in the 1920s when population grew to 250 by 1925. The town proudly displayed its mark of distinction on its main thoroughfare—

Tiger dredge and mine tailings, with sawmill, carpenter and machine shops.

fire hydrants.

The tight company town created its own society with its Tiger and Tigress Clubs. Their Thursday night free movies and Saturday evening dances drew a happy, harmonious crowd. Everyone stopped dancing the Charleston to join in a rallying chorus of the Tiger song, "Tiger, Oh, Tiger, live forever." Next morning, Sunday school took over the schoolhouse and later the town orchestra rehearsed. An idyllic life.

Chuck Chamberlain in a Frisco panel discussion decades later recalled his boyhood poverty in the 1920s. Most years his stocking hung limp and empty on Christmas morning. The family fortunes changed to "easy street" when Chamberlain's father snared a job at Tiger. They marveled over the luxury of electric lights and running water. (But Tiger still used outhouses.) As a family man, Chuck's father earned higher wages and rated better quarters (at $10 monthly rent) than singles. Sixty years later Chuck remembered food on the table and a heated home as "good" but he couldn't forget the best: a Christmas stocking bulging with toys and treats.

Meanwhile, the town's provident leader, John A. Traylor, pushed to achieve his impressive personal goal. Traylor played a millionaire's game similar to the board game, Monopoly, patented a few years later in 1933. To the Cashier and IXL, he added all the properties of the Tonopah Placers Company in 1926 for a mere $125,000. He snapped up

Tonopah's 58 placer and lode claims, plus all its water rights. He gained control of the Gold Pan Shops, by then called Tonopah Shops, and that company's three gold dredges. The dazzling Wellington-Oro Mine became his. He reached out and took the fabled Jessie and the legendary Wire Patch mines. Traylor's Royal Tiger Mines Company owned almost all Breckenridge area mining properties, dredges, and buildings on 8,315 famous acres. The company *became* mining in Summit County.

A fatal flaw brought his entire empire down. Though Traylor owned almost every foot of historically gold-seamed ground northeast of Breckenridge, that ground was dead. By 1929, the year of the Wall Street crash, 70 years of delving, burrowing, washing, scraping and scouring for gold left the land worked out. Traylor spent a then-astounding $2.7 million (when a restaurant dinner cost 25 cents) to develop mines already exhausted. Documents show that the company's total take between 1917 and 1931 came to a disappointing $109,000.

An unverified local story highlights the company's last-straw event: in 1930, shortly after the American stock market crashed, a thief stole $35,000 in company gold boxed for shipment next day to Denver's U.S. Mint. The Royal Tiger Mines, which had long lived on borrowed money and stock sales, had paid no income tax since 1928. In 1931, Traylor filed for bankruptcy.

Tiger town had lost 100 residents in 1929. Its school and library closed in 1933 and later so did its postoffice. Tiger slowly lapsed into a ghost town.

PIONEER PROFILE: John A. Traylor

John A. Traylor, the majordomo behind the Tiger mines and town, came from a colorful French family. Authorities in France deported Traylor's father, along with his brothers, for sheep rustling. The brothers, who spelled their name "Trailour," landed in Texas, where rustling also lacked popular acceptance.

Traylor, born in 1874, demonstrated leadership early in life. He spent his career in the west in mining-related jobs. He served as the young superintendent of Mexico's Calumet-Hecla Mine. He held a management post in Ely, Nevada in 1902-03 for the Nevada Consolidated Copper Company. Then he launched his own business, Traylor Engineering & Manufacturing in Salt Lake City.

A gifted administrator, entrepreneur and innovator, Traylor invented a shaker table used for concentrating ores, similar to Arthur Wilfley's ground-breaking 1895 Wilfley Table. His Traylor

Vibrator Company preceded a more extensive mine machinery manufacturing business which he spearheaded in Denver. There in 1907 he created John A. Traylor Machinery Company.

Traylor compensated for any personal flaws with self-confidence. He honed his talents. When unrest threatened in Mexico, he practiced shooting and became a crack shot. While working in Ely, Nevada, contention arose among unionized mine workers. A mine wage cut, accompanied by an increase in daily hours from eight to ten, enraged union workers. A gang of 25 had confronted Traylor hours earlier. Now a committee of five irate miners stormed into Traylor's office. When tension escalated, they advanced, one of them seizing Traylor by the shoulder. Traylor, the quick draw, reacted. In an instant, he pumped bullets into all five. Two lay wounded. Three miners died.

John Traylor (2nd from left) with wife, Tess, and the Martins at Tiger.

Traylor had a trail of successes but also faced notable disappointments. After purchasing the IXL's several lodes and mill site from friend, Thomas A. Brown, he made Brown a company board member and superintendent at the mine. Just a year after start-up in 1917, a dispute ended their working relationship. He then brought his brother, Edward, into the Tiger operation—another mistake. Edward sexually assaulted a 15-year old girl under his supervision. Though he fled Tiger before the birth of the girl's child, the 60-ish Edward Traylor was found, arrested and later faced trial. He died in prison in Canon City, Colorado in 1930, just before a dying Royal Tiger Mines Company declared bankruptcy.

John Traylor remained a strong family man who promoted family benefits at Tiger. He and his Southern-born wife, Tessie, had two children, Edna born in 1904 and John B., born in 1914. Young John grew up around mining and graduated from

Golden's respected Colorado School of Mines in 1936. He stood ready to step into his father's mining boots when, during his company's bankruptcy proceedings, the senior Traylor died November 20, 1937 at age 65.

John A. Traylor, like Thomas H. Fuller 50 years before him, acquired most of the stellar mining property around Breckenridge. Like Thomas Fuller in the 1870s, John Traylor not only owned mining in the 1920s, he *was* mining. The two historic figures, Fuller and Traylor, stand in Breckenridge history like sentinel peaks, the first at the beginning of mining as big business and the second at its demise.

Watch Out, Here Comes the Dredge!

One of the dredges acquired and lost by Traylor now aimed its gold-biting bucket-shaped teeth at the Blue River running through Breckenridge. The *Summit County Journal's* crusading editor, J.A. Theobald, railed against the company's insidious plan. "If we allow the dredge to make its cesspool ponds, and hideous tailings piles," Theobald contended, "we will have to apologize the remainder of our lives." He demanded that residents elect a new town government to replace the lax town board which failed to lift an eyelid in response to the dredge threat. When the Tonopah Placers Company, without permission, devoured the town's highway to the north, Theobald raged. "No individual has the right to destroy public property. Why a company?" he demanded. Theobald, himself a mining engineer, owned the *Journal* from 1911 to 1926, just when the dredge threat emerged. Born to write, he also published Denver's *Mineral Age,* a prominent mining journal and wrote a regular column for the *Denver Post.*

As the dredge inched toward Breckenridge's boundaries, the town board still dozed. "Buildings shake, windows rattle, houses have picture frames knocked off the walls by the concussion of the pounding gold boats," Theobald fumed. Dynamite charges catapulted boulders into homes, he complained. Yet the town did nothing.

The *Journal* editor scolded Tonopah attorney Barney Whatley. "When he has an opportunity of selling out to this dredge company he is willing to let the rest of the property owners suffer," Theobald charged. He exposed Tonopah's long-delayed and half-hearted attempt to repair the highway as "worse than a cow trail." He raised an outcry over the "mess of tailings piles left at Two Mile Bridge" on the river north of town, despite a public pledge to restore every unsightly scar. "One broken promise after another," Theobald groaned.

In early August 1923, citizens rallied to present a 50-signature petition to the town board opposing the dredge's entry to Breckenridge's residential core. On August 25, the dredge company's superintendent, J. E. Hopkins circulated his petition with a competing number of resident signatures supporting the dredge plan.

Tonopah Placers Company sidestepped citizen opposition by introducing a bill for an eminent-domain taking of the town's Blue River in the Colorado Legislature. The district's own senator, W. E. Renshaw, quietly brought the bill before the Senate. Ever alert, the *Journal's* Theobald caught wind of this polecat trick and raised an editorial stink. Renshaw withdrew the bill, protesting that Tonopah had misled him.

Nevertheless, the town finally granted permission for the Tonopah Dredge Company to cross the boundary into Breckenridge at its north end, on the old Hunt and Engle Placers. They extracted serious promises from Tonopah officials: fix the sewer system the company had destroyed and stop the town's raw sewage from pouring into the dredge pond and river; build a new crossing from the railroad tracks which now dangled over an open and dangerous dredge pathway; repair damaged highways; avoid wrecking the Watson Bridge; and more. Lawsuits followed failed agreements but early judges tended to find for companies. In response, Tonopah spearheaded a public relations program based on the ironic theme, "Industry is always to be preferred to scenic beauty."

Already beyond saving, historic Fort Mary B remains and the Jones Smelter lay crushed north of town in dredge-created ruins. The town's shrinking population could bring little opposition to the environmental disaster. The dredge company employed many of its citizens. Their salaries supported town businesses. Breckenridge-area dredging produced a half million dollars in gold during 1920 alone.

A glaring conflict of interest stood unchallenged: Breckenridge's mayor beginning in 1922, Trevor Thomas, held the job of dredge superintendent through the 1920s. (Sadly, he died in 1930. When a riverbank cave-in injured Thomas, he fell into the dredge pond and drowned.)

The dredge worked both day and night. Its buckets clanged and boulders crashed. Racket drowned family conversations and drummed out any sense of calm. When the noise stopped, however, residents couldn't sleep. It was too quiet.

In the end, Breckenridge fared better than its Swan Valley neighbor, Swan City, which a Bucyrus dredge crushed and obliterated in 1913.

Ski Tourney of the Century
Breckenridge needed a bright spot in the turbulent 1920s and found it. Peter Prestrud built a state-of-the-art ski jump on Lake Hill above Old Dillon. Norwegian Anders Haugen set a world record on that same Dil-

lon Jump in 1919. Now a February 29, 1920 ski tourney there drew 1,000 spectators who arrived on special ski trains from Denver, Leadville and Breckenridge (round-trip fare: $1.10). Anders Haugen thrilled the audience by exceeding his 1919 world record jump by one foot, a 214-foot feat. Universal Film Company photographers used moving -picture cameras to film the event. Spectators later rushed to Breckenridge's Eclipse Theater to see the movie, hoping to spot themselves in the crowd.

All that hoopla prompted Breckenridge to host its own ski jump tournament on Shock Hill just before the Dillon tournament. But balmy weather and hot sunshine created sticky snow and ruined the event. "A day for parasols," the *Journal* commented. Dillon's jump competition two days later faced the opposite problem: a blizzard blew in and too much snow spoiled the tourney.

Nevertheless, school children begged their parents for skis and homemade jumps marked many

Anders Haugen (l) and Peter Prestrud

hillsides. Ladies took ski outings. Men gathered on Sundays for jump competitions. Recreational skiing arrived in Breckenridge and came to stay.

Mining

The Wellington Mine provided a brief bright spot in 1920s Breckenridge. The decade began with the Wellington's mind-boggling $2.5 million dividend to stockholders. It yielded $11 million in mineral wealth by 1922. And zinc, the mine's strong suit, out-produced dredge gold in 1920, with $570,000 in output, $70,000 more than dredging's $500,000.

However a 1920s decline in mineral prices, especially in the Wellington's ace mineral, zinc, caused the mine to lay off most of its workforce. The June 7, 1924 move "cast a gloom over Breckenridge," the *Journal* intoned, because the mainstay mine ranked as the town's top employer and thus drove dollars to many town businesses.

The decade ended with the Royal Tiger Mines Company's purchase of the Wellington. By March 1, 1929 the failing Tiger operation had pulled the pumps and all valuable equipment from the Wellington. On March 15, Breckenridge's best mine, the Wellington, flooded.

In 1922 the Reiling Dredge, recently purchased for $50,000 and overhauled by new owners, suffered a heavy ice buildup that caused the boat to sink in its own pond. The 1909-launched dredge never worked again. Also Ben Stanley Revett's 1905 Reliance dredge, now owned by the Tonopah Placers Company, shut down in 1920. So by 1923, only two dredges operated, both on the Blue River.

Always ready to tout mining's success, not its downturns, the *Journal* trumpeted a $10,000 silver strike at Indiana Gulch's Warriors Mark Mine, a silvery Christmas present to a sinking mining industry. The story earned a December, 1921 page-one five-column banner headline.

Transportation Woes

In 1929 the stock market crashed. The Colorado & Southern, plagued by dwindling ore freight profits, added its own bad news to the crash gloom. The railway on September 20, 1929 again threatened Breckenridge with its plan to abandon service to the town. The Chamber of Commerce, organized to oppose the railroad's plans to shut down almost two decades earlier, circulated a petition of protest that bore 575 signatures. Breckenridge managed again to postpone rail closure.

More and more, the community banded together to shovel out Hoosier Pass each spring, an arduous task. Late snow often prevented opening the all-important pass till mid-June.

Loveland Pass, an alternate route, had fallen into disrepair after stagecoach days ended. But the *Journal* announced, "a car made it over Loveland Pass," on October 11, 1929. Road crews worked on the east side to restore the old trail and crews would soon tackle Loveland's west side to open a much-needed alternative access to the outside world.

The 1920s witnessed dwindling mining returns, declining dredge profits and the rise of skiing as a recreational and competitive sport. Again Breckenridge shifted, this time to face a still-distant future. The mining industry lay behind. Skiing as an industry lay ahead—but its reality loomed on a distant horizon. Meanwhile, the Great Depression of the 1930s, the war years of the 1940s and the new hope of the late 1950s began to materialize, like clouds of change enveloping the jagtoothed Ten Mile peaks in mist.

11

1930s – 1950s

The '30s were awful rough," Frank Brown said in a June 10, 1988 *Summit County Journal* interview, "but I miss my old friends—everyone was my friend. That's how we were in those days."

Frank, who married his wife Theta in 1928, summed up the character of 1930s-1950s Breckenridge: an oversized family that gathered in grizzled miners, aging pioneers, strong widows, poor young marrieds, a few rascals and an exceptional literary couple.

The eclectic population had to stick together. Times were lean and winters hard.

Main Street, State Highway 9, collected three-foot deep snow in winter before the state plow came. After plowing, the road quickly became impassible again. Frank Brown reminisced:

You could shoot a cannon down Main Street and never hit anyone. The streets were lit with what seemed like 10-watt bulbs—although I know they had to be brighter than that—they were really dark, the streets were graveled and there were some sidewalks, not many.

And the main water system would freeze up every winter. It was a nightmare when the water mains froze up. For eight months I had to carry water from the river in one of them old, long bathtubs.

Frank and Theta Brown

When the 1930s Depression drove the shrinking mine town into economic despair, lot prices dropped to $5. Some homeowners, unable to pay property tax, tried to give their houses away. They found no takers.

Yet the gulches came alive with gold seekers. They jerry-rigged hydraulic pipe to once again carry water. They fashioned homemade rockers and repaired cabins. Men desperate to feed their families came to the Breckenridge gold fields in the 1930s to mine.

Frank and Theta Brown
Frank Brown, who lived in Breckenridge over 65 years, held longtime elected positions as town mayor for 18 years and county treasurer for 34 years. "When I was mayor, there wasn't anything going on," he admitted. "It was really dead around here." (He doesn't mention the ruckus surrounding his 1946 mayoral election when he had to go to court to secure a win over opponent Robert Theobald.) During the decades he served as county treasurer, Frank's garrulous conversational gifts served him well in political life. Theta, who worked for years as his deputy, declared, "I did all the work and Frank did all the talking."

Frank beat longtime treasurer George Robinson for the county position in 1940. The vote tally, published in the *Journal* reveals a bleak precinct voter count: Brown, 33; Robinson 15.

Theta, born in the Breckenridge residence at 225 South Main Street, attended high school in the brick school building on Harris Street. Always an exuberant personality, she professed to have at least one boyfriend for every year of school. She loved big hats, pretty dresses, dancing, horses and bowling. Her vivacious nature earned her the title, Sweetheart of Breckenridge. In her younger years, she roamed the flower-carpeted slopes above town. "It was beautiful here," she remembered in an April 8, 1993 *Breckenridge Journal* interview. "There was no skiing (corporation) and I picked mushrooms and black currants. I loved horses and I rode the donkeys. They ran around Breckenridge," she said, referring to the pack animals abandoned after mining days ended. After World War II, she drove around in a battered jeep.

In her older years, Theta, tiny but tenacious, showed up at the Breckenridge Inn for bowling league night "armed for bear." She arrived ready to take on any challenger. A champion bowler, she traveled to events in other states to compete.

Theta Brown died in 1993. Frank followed her in 1994.

Old pioneers passed away, including Martha Silverthorn Finding, who died in 1931. A young breed of individuals then made up the town. One of these, Sena Otterson Valaer, started life on a ranch down the Blue. Her family bought the beautiful Forman house at 100 North High Street after she graduated from high school in Breckenridge. In an era of silk stockings and art deco, Sena learned to create the tight, stylized waves of the cropped 1930s hairstyle and earned spending money doing hair for Breckenridge ladies.

A lady far too busy for tedious marcel waving, Miss Susan Badger, served as county welfare director. A refugee from aristocratic Eastern society, she found jobs for unemployed Depression-era workers, mended marriages, collected wages for unpaid laborers, performed funerals for welfare babies who died and listened for untold hours to the woes of persons on public assistance—all for $276.37 per month. She also played a mean hand of poker, smoked cigars and drank whiskey straight. Her life took a tragic turn when her fiancé, died before their wedding. She considered herself a fugitive from her ancestors. Of Breckenridge, she said in a profile written by friend and author Helen Rich, "Here I can be myself."

Homemade Bread and Whiskey

Helen Rich and her partner Belle Turnbull roamed ghost towns, climbed

Miner Curly Mackie, an illiterate French St. neighbor, drove highly literate Helen (l.) and Belle to ghost mine towns in his jeep. They absorbed local lore.

crags above timberline to view old mines and absorbed into their bones the scent of spruce sap, the icy chill of forest shade, the sheer stagger of morning sun lighting the Ten Mile peaks. They drank in miners' tales like spring water and devoured stories of lives lived too close to the sky. Of these they wrote, Belle in poetry and poetic prose, and Helen in salty, picturesque stories.

The Ladies of French Street, as Breckenridge called them, cultivated a passion for high mountains and quirky mountain folk since their 1938 arrival. Belle's poetry in *The Tenmile Range* and *Goldboat* penetrates mountain life like a Tenmile Range jag tooth pierces the sky. Helen's *The Willowbender* and *The Spring Begins* capture the character of people—young wives in isolated cabins insane from winter loneliness and prospectors so gold-sick that obsession became a mountain kind of crazy.

The literate ladies chopped their own wood for a Franklin Stove in a no-plumbing cabin on French Street. They entertained aging madams, tale-telling miners and celebrated poets like Colorado poet laureate, Tom Ferril, and Pulitzer prize winning author, Bernard Devoto. Robert Cooper, a boy who perched on a stool while guests munched Helen's homemade bread and drank whiskey, told this author that he came away wide-eyed.

Helen Rich, who shrank from party chatter but loved intelligent conversation, chopped firewood for exercise and called poker and fishing her two hobbies. Her fishing license, she lamented, indicated that she had no distinguishing characteristics. Yet Breckenridge regarded the former newswoman, now clad in flannel shirts and a French beret, as a distinguished resident.

Belle Turnbull

The dainty Belle Turnbull confided that Vassar never taught her how to break trail on snowshoes (she called them "webs,") or how to get rid of pack rats or how to hang a haunch of venison. But her unsentimental Scotch background made her spare with words and brought a lean brilliance to her poetry.

The two women rejected the romantic past of their fading mine camp and wrote of the granite-and-gneiss harshness of current life in the Colorado Rockies.

A man who knew that harshness, Alva Springmeyer, lived through Breckenridge's lean years. A November 11, 1993 article published on his death, reveals his hardships. He remembered the work in the mines, the lean times after the mines closed, the isolation after Breckenridge lost the railroad. Earlier, when coal cars freighted in coal for the mines, the townspeople gathered spilled coal along the tracks. But after the railway quit, a strict unwritten rule limited gathering to one paper sack of coal per family per day. Families endured chilly houses.

Because he had a gas station, Alva Springmeyer saw customers struggle to get a dollar for gasoline. Men would offer him title to their trucks to trade for some gas and a couple of dollars in cash. In 1930, the entire county issued only 314 auto license tags. Springmeyer reckoned that it snowed more in the old days. Sometimes he shoveled eight feet of snow so his wife, Aggie, could cross the street to open the store she owned. Men got started at 5 a.m. snow shoveling to be ready for the work day.

No Man's Land

Despite poverty, Breckenridge people knew how to have fun. Prohibition, repealed in 1933, no longer squashed the party scene. The celebration of No Man's Land in 1936 provided an excuse for a shindig that drew Colorado Governor "Big Ed" Johnson and other dignitaries to the new "kingdom of Breckenridge." Town land, considered by a group of local ladies to be left out of the Louisiana Purchase, became its own fiefdom. No Man's Land celebrated Breckenridge's re-entry into the United States. No matter that the facts failed to jibe with actual history. State historian LeRoy R. Hafen informed the ladies that a 1919 treaty had re-

First No Man's Land drew Gov. Ed Johnson (l.)

solved the problem. Dreary mid-1930s Breckenridge, however, reveled in the chance for an annual party.

To mark the twelfth No Man's Land anniversary, August 7-8, 1948, a full program of horse races and carnival events, including stunt riding and calf roping, culminated in the unusual feat of square dancing on horseback. But the stellar attraction, a widely-known "shimmy queen" named Gilda Gray, stole the fete as queen of the event's firemen's ball. Since none of these festivities could be conducted dry, the exhilarating effect of mountain air combined with other stimulants made the celebration one remembered with happy nostalgia.

Another diversion from economic woes took advantage of Summit County's exceptional snow. During the 1930s through the 1950s locals spearheaded new ski courses which foreshadowed the 1960 introduction of the Breckenridge Ski Area.

Rope Tow to Heaven

Breckenridge historian and author Maureen Nicholls in a March 19, 2008 presentation chronicled the Hoosier Pass Ski Course. Her story: the South Park Lions Club wanted to build a ski run near the Hoosier summit. Its sole challenge: winter access. The 1930s roads even in town rarely saw a plow. Snow piled up on Hoosier Pass all winter, and blocked the road. In late May and June, crews, sometimes aided by a two-horse team and crude plow, shoveled it clear. But in 1937, the Colorado Highway Department constructed a building to house their rotary snowplow (one just like the railroad used but on wheels) and took over maintaining Hoosier Pass road. Ski enthusiasts rushed to install a rope tow in 1937 and saw their reward with a crowd of 500 exultant skiers. Early Ford, Chevrolet and Dodge cars jammed the summit parking and roadway, frustrating highway officials. So the ski course moved to a new site below the Bemrose Mine with room for parking. They used Bemrose mine cabins for skier sleeping quarters. Soon the Hoosier Pass Club opened, offering a bar, complete with juke box, dining and lodging. Breckenridge's first ski resort, now a full-service facility, awaited international fame.

It came. A globe-trotting ski entourage arrived in January, 1938 according to the January 7, *Summit County Journal*. They came because of sparse snow at the Broadmoor Hotel, their luxurious ski destination. Count Phillipe de Fret of Belgium, Merrell Fanone of New York City, Walter Abel of Baltimore and Nice, France, and eight other 1930s glitterati created headline news when they skied Hoosier Pass. The area's two north-facing runs, separated by a tree island, provided top-quality snow.

Lesser mortals used the rope tow at the 1939 Blue Valley Ski Course at Carter Park. When the U.S. entered World War II, skiing there stopped because no able men were available to run the tow. But after the war in 1948, Breckenridge fire department volunteers brought in a motor and transformed some Montezuma mine-tram equipment to update the tow. They also installed lights for night skiing. In 1948-50 the hill stayed open two nights a week. Many local youngsters learned to ski at Carter Park. Local instructors there, including Summit County ski legend Edna Dercum, put small skiers onto used U.S. Army Tenth Mountain Division skis, painted white for camouflage.

Finally, starting in the 1940s, Peak 10 drew a merry group of summer skiers to its July snowfields.

Rail Shutdown

During the 1930s Depression, Breckenridge reached a low point. The

Engine 9 on Georgetown Loop

Colorado & Southern railway shut down in 1937, after years of threats and actual attempts to do so. The closure cut a lifeline to mountain-sequestered Summit County and a severed vital link to the outside world for Breckenridge. Loss of rail service also crippled transportation within Summit County. Without plowed roads, cars went up on blocks for winter storage. Instead of driving, people rode the C&S. Dillon terminated high school classes the year the railroad quit. Students traveled by school bus to the high school in Breckenridge. (Don't think snappy yellow school bus. Think carbon monoxide-endangered dump truck.) Here's what former student Chick Deming wrote in an August 11, 2008 letter to the author:

The school bus was a converted dump truck, the dump part being removed and an old-old school bus body bolted to the frame. The bus part held about 10-12 kids. Access was through a back door. Heat was supplied from the engine by the exhaust pipe running through the enclosure. A bench was constructed over the exhaust pipe. You can't imagine how hot the pipe was. In later years I marveled that we kids weren't asphyxiated. On cold days we all huddled around the exhaust pipe.

PIONEER PROFILE: E. C. Peabody

As a boy, Elmer Clifton Peabody oozed mischief.

His mother, Almeda Peabody, ran the Colorado House, a Ridge Street boardinghouse still standing at 106 South Ridge Street. She stayed busy, preparing homemade foods for her fine table and laundering muslin sheets. So Cliff, as he was called, had the freedom to meet other boys at an abandoned mine cabin at Yuba Dam Flats, where French Creek meets the Blue just north of Breckenridge. An in-crowd of six or so boys brought sweets, coffee and a coffee pot and had an all-dessert picnic in the cabin. They could buy a dozen doughnuts for ten cents, a lemon pie for 20 cents, and a pound of Arbuckle's coffee (the best brand) for 20 cents. The boys devoured these goodies until they raised a sufficient sugar and caffeine high to begin their pranks.

One of the group's rites of initiation involved cruising the hillsides to find a boulder positioned in a direct line above an old mine cabin. The boy undergoing testing would roll the boulder in hopes of gaining a direct hit to demolish the log cabin. One escapade targeted a shack inhabited by Tom Abbott, a drifter who moved from cabin to cabin. Each building the man lived in ended in flames, torched by old Tom.

The boys didn't dream of the moment of glory awaiting them when they put their shoulders to a big round stone above Tom's present abode. In his granddaughter's history, *Pioneer Voices*, Peabody remembered:

> *Just as the boulder reached the cabin it struck a log or another large boulder and bounced into the air. Then it landed on the roof of the cabin and fell inside. Little did we suspect that "Old Tom" was inside. When he came running out, it was every boy for himself. I personally never made it to town before that day, or after it, in so short a time.*

Cliff, born on Christmas Day, 1884, moved to Breckenridge with his family at age 6 in 1891. His father, Edwin, was a brother of Leland Peabody, the 1859er who long drew placer gold riches from Gold Run Gulch and later from his Peabody Placer near South Park's neighbor towns, Tarryall and Hamilton.

Fourteen years old when the Big Snow Winter buried Breckenridge, Cliff took in all the details. He later wrote a valuable record published serially in the 1954 *Summit County Journal*. As a teenager, he took dancing lessons along with all the other youth. He donned a tuxedo, a cutaway or Prince Albert coat with white dress vest and shiny shoes to attend the elegant dances that crowned 1900s Breckenridge social life. Later he left home for San Francisco and managed to survive the city disintegration around him during the 1906 earthquake. Firemen stood helpless beside broken water mains as fire after the quake engulfed remaining buildings.

Cliff returned to Breckenridge to marry Victoria Rosedahl, a young Summit County high school teacher. Their only child, Elmer Clifton, Jr., was born in 1912 at their home at 303 North Main Street.

Cliff, now a father, worked for the productive Wellington Mine as a hoist man and earned enough to buy a ranch along the Lower Blue ten miles north of today's Silverthorne. When their son reached age five, the couple

E. C. Peabody

moved to the ranch full time. Through the years, Cliff Peabody held better and better mining jobs, including a post as superintendent both for Kokomo's prestigious Wilfley Mine and Fairplay's London Mine. He also won election in the 1930s as county clerk and recorder and served on a wartime draft board.

When Old Dillon had to moe its cemetery for the coming dam and reservoir, officials chose E. C. Peabody to handle the difficult and politically-delicate task of researching the deceased and obtaining permission from relatives to move their graves.

A hard worker, he made his Columbine Ranch self-sufficient. He generated his own electricity with a wind charger and glass batteries. He also operated his own blacksmith forge and maintained an on-site vehicle repair garage. He built a heated swimming pool with its own outside boiler for his adored granddaughters and flooded a skating area for their winter fun. The girls, who called him "Pags," listened to tales of his youthful exploits, which he told with a mixture of pride and embarrassment. His granddaughter, Sally, recalled that he never raised his voice. "He never said a mean world to my Grandma."

Years of mining deteriorated E.C. Peabody's lungs. He died of tuberculosis in a Denver care center on March 6, 1956 at age 70.

E.C. Peabody earned the respect of Breckenridge and Summit County. His life spanned the years from Breckenridge's affluent 1890s through his homespun 1950s ranch days. A man conscious of history in the making, Elmer Clifton Peabody left his stamp. His "E.C. Peabody Remembers" columns and his record of the Big Snow Winter have painted our grayscale picture of early Breckenridge with vivid color.

Wartime Breckenridge

As the 1940s approached, Hitler's dark cloud shrouded Europe in war. In 1941 when Japan attacked Hawaii's Pearl Harbor, America entered World War II. Breckenridge boys enlisted. Some entered harm's way. For example, the C. P. Enyearts' son, Loren, became a German prisoner at Stalag III near Luckenwulde, Germany. Others returned wounded. Several Summit County boys died.

On October 15, 1942 War Production Board Order L-203 brought all gold mining to an abrupt halt. Dredge jobs ended. None of this stopped a patriotic Summit County from exceeding its war bond quota by 112 percent.

Breckenridge residents were so poor that they almost didn't feel the pinch of wartime rationing. If they could afford to shop, they could purchase only four gallons of gasoline; one pound of coffee; and one pair of shoes per month. Housewives studied newspaper tips on how to sweeten without sugar, except during canning season when families could get a rare five pounds of sugar. Rationing also applied to processed foods. In the 1940s this meant canned goods.

War-weary Americans endured sending their sons to battle and curtailing their wants. But the nation grieved for its president, Franklin D. Roosevelt, when he died of polio in April, 1945. The *Journal's* front page mourned his loss in multiple front-page stories on his death.

Stinging winters lashed out through the 1940s, buffeting Breckenridge with high winds, blizzards, snowslides and bitter cold. These built up to the record-breaking winter of 1949-50 when snow buried Breckenridge, isolated the town from the outside and caused a spring runoff that ripped through gulches and turned the Blue River into a torrent. Denver experienced devastating floods in spring, with loss of life and property.

Snow saved the day when a robber raced from town up Hoosier Pass with his loot. The felon hit the brakes when traffic backed up due to an avalanche. After crews cleared the road, officers checked each auto at the summit and let each one pass—except car number 10, whose driver went to jail.

Prices in the 1940s seemed high then but appear cheap today. Chicken fryers sold for 41 cents a pound. Halibut steaks cost 45 cents a pound. And T-bone or Porterhouse steak was a bargain at 39 cents a pound.

Mrs. McAbee

A woman whose cheery voice and take-charge personality boosted Breckenridge spirits in the 1940s was Metta McAbee. Mrs. McAbee manned telephone central as chief operator for the town's Mountain State Telephone Company service. For twenty-three years, Mrs. McAbee's melodious "Number, please?" and quick response to help made picking up the telephone a pleasure. When the hearse motored down Main Street, callers asked her who died. When the sheriff entered the courthouse, the curious called to ask "Is somebody in trouble?" Questions such as "What time is it?" and "Where's the fire?" and "My baby's sick. Who should I call?" prompted a kind and speedy response from Metta McAbee.

A loyal member of St. John's Episcopal Church, which provided this information, she was also a radio fan. She became acquainted with Denver's radio greats. Radio personalities like Chuck Collins, Starr Yelland and Bill Barker regularly mentioned Metta McAbee. Her 1951 retirement, celebrated in style at the old Brown Hotel on Ridge Street, coincided with the introduction of a new telephone dial system. Residents lamented the loss of Mrs. McAbee's welcoming voice.

The town entered the 1950s rejoicing that the county paved some local roads for the first time ever. In a 1980s interview story by Jean Lannan, resident Martha Enyeart said,

Despite the fact that Breckenridge was almost a ghost town, there were always several grocery stores here. As for clothing, auto parts and other necessities of life, Lege's General Store in Dillon was it.

Her husband, Carl, added that Breckenridge lacked a dentist for 45 years. People just endured a toothache. Medical care presented a challenge. A 1950s hospital board raised $40,000 on a bond issue to build a clinic but the project failed when federal regulations required a full-time dietician and an expensive oxygen storage center.

Community will, however, remained strong. Enyeart remembered:

There was a great sense of community spirit. People, with a few exceptions, were living on a survival level. One had to make his or her own fun. Box lunches, socials and dances were common events in which everyone participated—from grandparents to babes-in-arms.

Folksy 1940s and 50s drew townspeople together for parades and parties.

Breckenridge, 100 years old in 1959, celebrated its first century with beards for the men, six shooters, Western gear and burros. As 100 years earlier in the 1859 gold discovery year, Breckenridge now stood poised on the brink of a boom. In 1860, placer gold drew thousands over the skyscraping Continental Divide. Now Breckenridge's alpine winters, its snow-blanketed slopes, its mine camp heritage combined to schuss the town into new growth beginning in 1960—with world-class skiing.

12

1960s – Present

Breckenridge reached its century mark in 1959 poised like a skier, ready to plunge into a long, double diamond run. The initial descent proved exhilaratingly steep. Along the way mogul fields, rocky spots and double fall lines raised adrenalin. But the 50-year ride took tiny Breckenridge to national, even world, prominence.

Breckenridge skiing, long a local tradition, entered its own on December 17, 1961 when Breckenridge ski area opened. Instead of a last gasp, the near-ghost town population gave a collective sigh of relief.

The Peak 8 ski venture emerged as a result of the connection between key players—Bill Rounds, Bill Stark, Sigurd Rockne and Trygve Berge.

Bill Rounds, part of Wichita's family-owned Rounds & Porter Lumber Company, became a 1950s ski enthusiast. His pal, Whip Jones, helped to develop Aspen Highlands. While skiing at Aspen, Rounds met two tanned and athletic Norwegian transplants, Sigurd Rockne and Trygve Berge. Rounds struck up a friendship with the former Norway ski champs, then Aspen Highlands ski instructors.

1960s Breckenridge, a ghost town ready for resurrection.

Meanwhile, Rounds' colleague, geologist Bill Stark, scouted land around Breckenridge for mining claims. Instead he found development land. News of Vail's coming ski mountain and creation of the tourist-draw Dillon Reservoir had leaked out. Stark's report to Bill Rounds convinced him that Summit County stood ready to jump start development. He launched a branch of his lumber business in Breckenridge to provide materials for vacation homes around the new Lake Dillon. He hired Rockne and Berge to build Antrim Lumber, later called Breckenridge Building Center.

The Rounds family organized another new company, Summit County Development Corporation (SCDC) and began buying up Breckenridge land. The company gained 5,500 acres for an average price of $55 per acre. Trygve and Sigurd, ever the ski proponents, raved over the ski mountain potential of Breckenridge's Peak 8. The threesome made a summer jeep trip up the peak where the men toasted the peak's possibilities with Cutty Sark and icy water from a spring. A Peak 8 winter jaunt, aided by a Kristi snowcat for the ascent, provided the men a powder ski down that sold Rounds on the peak's dry fluffy snow and varied terrain. The ski mountain plan took off.

Rounds & Porter launched Summit County Development Corporation with Claude Martin, a Wichita Rounds executive, and Bill Stark at its helm. Almost immediately, Breckenridge saw benefits. The company developed the Weisshorn, Coyne Valley and Bekkedal subdivisions. It shouldered infrastructure costs, including a new town water and sewer system. SCDC spent more than $60,000 to improve Breckenridge before the ski mountain debuted, according to a November, 1961 Cervi's *Rocky Mountain Journal*, a Colorado business newspaper. In a politically-motivated move, officials condemned Breckenridge's historic brick schoolhouse in 1962. So Rounds and Porter offered the town a 30-acre site for a new school. They threw in a $10,000 library and a three-acre hospital site. But Mayor Frank Brown and his wife Theta, along with a small horde of others, loved bowling. Brushing aside the other community benefits, they asked for, and got, a fine new bowling alley.

In rapid-fire succession, the new ski area group submitted an application to the U.S. Forest Service in March, 1961, received its approval July 27, 1961 and opened its ski mountain on December 17, 1961. A road up Peak 8, a Heron double chairlift and T-bar, the Bergenhof cafeteria, a ticket office and a lodge for visitors called the Breckenridge Inn, rose almost overnight. All this construction happened despite a huge September snowstorm that challenged progress.

No setback or obstacle slowed the advance of the Peak 8 Ski Area toward its December, 1961 target date. On opening day, the Heron double chairlift whisked skiers 1,400 feet up Peak 8. 17,000 skiers paid $4 per ticket to ski that first season. Ski area manager Ken Cotton oversaw a mountain operation that included a ski school with Sigurd and Trygve as directors; a ski patrol headed by Don Bachman; and a base area including parking, the new Bergenhof and ticket office-administration building.

That same busy building on January 10, 1966 exploded due to a butane gas leak which ignited when a furnace came on. Children in the nursery escaped harm but one skier died and others sustained serious injuries. Roy McGinnis, a surveyor, who was eating lunch inside remembered the sound "like a jet dove on us." Jim Nicholls, a ski instructor, recalled that the well-built roof flew off in once piece, then fell back onto the blown-apart building forcing out the air and effectively squashing a tragic fire. Nicholls' eyes get teary forty-plus years later talking about it.

A lesser but amusing hazard lay in the January, 1962-installed T-bar which occasionally hooked and ripped skiers' jackets. One day the unpredictable T-bar snagged a woman's sweater and pealed it off her body, right down to her bra.

The T-bar succumbed to a succession of new lifts during the late 1960s. Skier numbers increased. But empty slopes in January bothered the Norwegians. So they pitched a plan for a January, 1964 festival, Ullr Dag, designed to draw skiers. A parade, competitions, and aerial flips by Trygve—notable today because skiers accomplished these feats on 215 centimeter skis—attracted crowds to a celebration that continues each January today.

From a humble start at Peak 8, today's Breckenridge Ski Resort emerged.

Dr. John Smith attended injuries in Breckenridge. For the more serious cases, a Cadillac hearse that doubled as the Summit County ambulance transported patients to Denver.

The ski patrol began with seat-of-the-pants training. Nick Payne recalled in a 2002 *Breckenridge Magazine* article by Claudia Carbone the day in the 1970s that his boss told him to try skiing with a patrol toboggan. "I pulled Ted Zawora down Park Lane and got going too fast," Payne remembered. "I didn't know how to stop. Ted bailed and I blew up down the road."

The ski area continued through the 1970s, an era when hippies invaded Breckenridge. The 1970s also brought plans for the town's first supermarket, City Market. Still, Main Street sported so many empty lots that it rivaled a seven-year old's toothless smile. But the mellow 1970s ushered in a hefty list of ski area accomplishments.

Ski Area Time Line

Business developments through the mountain's nearly 50 years include:

1970   Aspen Ski Corporation buys Breckenridge.

1971   Peak 9 opens.

1975-76   Breckenridge attracts one-half million skiers. Ski School staff increases to 100 instructors.

1978   Aspen Ski Corporation, including Breckenridge, sells to Twentieth Century-Fox Film Corporation. That company, long on cash due to Star Wars profits, invests in various enterprises and gives Breckenridge its first non-ski owner. In August, 1978 Colorado's first Alpine Slide opens.

1980-81   A drought year limits snow. The mountain opens for three days at Christmas and closes until mid-February. The world's first high speed quad chair lift is installed on Peak 9.

1981-82 $2.5 million pays for snowmaking equipment on Peak 9 to combat poor snowfall. That season the ski area gets a whopping 217 inches. The world's first high-speed detachable quad chairlift debuts, feted by a parade and a 10-piece brass band in costume from Austria.

1983-84   Breckenridge hosts the Michelin World Freestyle Invitational and the Hawaiian Tropic Celebrity Pro-Am—the first World Cup points freestyle competition held in the U.S. Breckenridge becomes the first major ski resort in Colorado to allow snowboarding.

1985   Peak 10 opens, interconnecting three mountain peaks of ski terrain. The resort hosts the world's first Snowboarding World

Cup race. Lift #1 retires after 25 years of service, replaced by the Colorado Super Chair, a high speed quad. An avalanche in the then out-of-bounds Peak 7 bowl takes four young lives. On the corporate side, Twentieth Century-Fox sells its 50% Breckenridge holdings to the Bell Mountain Partnership. The other 50% now belongs to Miller-Klutznick-Davis-Gray, a Chicago real estate partnership.

1987-88 Breckenridge hits the one million mark in skier visits. On June 30, 1988, Japan's Victoria Company, Ltd. of Tokyo purchases Breckenridge. A subsidiary of a Japanese sporting goods store chain, the new Victoria-Breckenridge Ski Corporation places Kaz Sakaguchi in charge.

1989-90 Sakaguchi floats a $75 million, 10-year expansion plan, not yet fully realized, to include skiing on Peaks 7 and 6, plus a cable car train lift to a revolving restaurant at the top of Peak 8. Imperial Bowl opens to the public.

1991-92 Alpine World Cup slalom and GS races take place at Breckenridge for the first time. Lift ticket prices rise to $36.

1993 The Ralston Purina Company purchases the Breckenridge ski area and selected real estate assets from Victoria U.S.A.

1993-94 No longer out of bounds, the Peak 7 Bowl opens to skiers.

1996 Ralcorp merges with New York City's Apollo Group, the parent company of Keystone, Arapahoe Basin, Vail, Beaver Creek and Arrowhead. Wall Street now owns regional skiing. The new company, Vail Resorts, which will later divest Arapahoe Basin, foresees running the largest ski resort complex in North America.

2003 Vail Resorts becomes a public company. Apollo's Rob Katz will take over as CEO and later board chairman.

2004-05 Peak 7 terrain opens with gentle runs. The Imperial Express Chairlift opens as the highest lift in North America at 12,840 feet giving access to steep-chutes ski terrain.

2006 Breckenridge, America's most popular ski area, hosts 1.65 million skier visits.

2007 Breckenridge launches the BreckConnect Gondola, which whisks skiers from in-town parking lots to Peak 8 skiing.

2009 The community studies Breckenridge's proposal for wildland, back-country lift-served ski development in first-growth forest on Peak 6. Day ticket price reaches $92.

PIONEER PROFILE: Jim and Maureen Nicholls

Jim and Maureen Nicholls straddle the era from 1961 to the present day. They have one foot stationed in early 1960s Breckenridge. It was then a town of 250 peopled by miners' widows living in shabby Victorian homes and washed-up prospectors, their eyes milky with cataracts, reminiscing at the Gold Pan. The other foot they have planted in an emerging Breckenridge ski town that hurtled forward into nonstop development and became a first-class year-round resort community.

Jim and Maureen Nicholls

Jim helped scope land use options at the base while the Peak 8 ski mountain took shape. He taught skiing there. Maureen volunteered for ski patrol. Today Jim owns Cowboy Stuff, a cowboy-Indian antique gallery, and Maureen acts as the town's one-woman historical archive. Both have involved themselves in Breckenridge, living its history and creating history along the way.

Nearly 50 years ago, the two young transplants received a warm welcome from Breckenridge's long-time residents. "The old people loved seeing young adults come to work in a new industry, one that would keep them here," Maureen comments. "And they loved seeing children on the streets, things they remembered from earlier days."

Jim arrived first in 1961, seeking land for his parents' retirement home. He stopped at Main Street's Summit County Development Corporation and met Claude Martin, manager. "Who sits there?" Jim inquired, pointing to an empty drafting table. "No one," replied Martin. Jim filled that desk chair 15 days later.

The fading town "had windows out," Jim recalls, "and curtains flying in the breeze." Incongruous, he says, but it was "a booming ghost town."

Jim already had roots in the rocky soil of the Colorado high country. His great-grandfather came to Colorado in 1878, mining in the Ten Mile Canyon, where big silver strikes occurred in 1878, and also in mushrooming Leadville and later bonanza Cripple Creek. Though Jim grew up in Gary, Indiana, he spent vacations in Colorado and chose Fort Collins for college. When Jim came back to Breckenridge to start his new job, a Labor Day snowstorm that deposited three feet of snow in town and five feet on the mountain didn't faze him.

But the challenge of making Breckenridge's name known might have fazed him. Jim worked on promotion, design and artwork for advertising materials that presented to the public eye an unknown Peak 8 Ski Area above an obscure former mining town.

One of his assignments involved creating a sign to post at the junction of Colorado highways 6 and 40, before I-70 was built. "No one knew where the town was." He created a six-foot sign with the imposing word, Breckenridge, painted on it, along with a large arrow. It looked just like an official highway sign. "We went down there in the middle of the night and planted that sign. It stayed there for four or five years."

Michigan-born Maureen Sloan, who set a goal as a teenager to someday live in Colorado, moved to Colorado Springs as a teacher in 1963. She made frequent ski trips to Breckenridge. A skier since age four, she took and passed the National Ski Patrol exam and volunteered for weekend duty at the newly-renamed Breckenridge Ski Area. (The new name helped skiers realize where Peak 8 was.)

Jim, a ski instructor, and Maureen, a patroller, met, got engaged on a Peak 8 chairlift and in 1966 married, all within five months. Maureen skied for seven months while pregnant with their first child. Finally, patrollers hid her boots to make her quit. "Everyone on the mountain made bets about which ski run the baby would be named for," she said. "Mach 1 Nicholls, or Tiger Nicholls?"

Soon Maureen found herself pushing a baby buggy up Breckenridge's rough roadways and chatting with the old-timers every chance she got. She always loved older people. When they needed help, the Nicholls both gave it, cleaning barns, painting, fixing roofs and organizing garage sales. She began to see old cookstoves, carbide lamps, silver collections and documents disappearing from Breckenridge. Likewise, historic buildings, dredge tailings, and mine-era buildings such as the ruins of the bawdy house, the Blue Goose, all faced destruction.

"When I saw this, I got interested in preservation," she recalls. So with two blonde toddler girls, Kristie and Carrie, in tow, she worked with others in 1968 to start the Summit Historical Society. She served first as secretary, then as president for seven years. A third daughter, Jill, arrived in fall, 1973, the year the Society opened its Dillon museum. The Society's best achievement, however, came at the time of Breckenridge's centennial as an incorporated town, 1980, when the group completed the creation of the town's National Historic District. This 250-building district ranks as one of Colorado's largest.

Maureen also zeroed in on historic photographs, the fading and cracked images of a vanishing past. Colorado Mountain College in the 1970s excelled in photography courses. Maureen learned, operated her own darkroom and brought old images alive. Four major collections came into her hands. She used them to create a unique and historic picture library.

A neighbor gave Maureen a carton of 1,000 Brownie box camera negatives taken by early 1900s photo enthusiast, Minnie Thomas. Another offered Maureen several boxes of antique glass plate negatives from her attic. "Ninety-three out of 96 plates were of Breckenridge," Maureen remembers with glee. And a third stash of historic photo gems fell at her feet with three albums of Otto Westerman's 1890s images. He worked as the official photographer of the South Park railroad. Finally, in the early 1990s, she received a collection of turn-of-the-century Breckenridge panoramas.

"A cute old man, whose ill-fitting false teeth clicked," came to her, wanting copies of historic railroad pictures. Maureen provided them at no charge. Later the man returned the favor with his gift of the priceless panoramas. She created her book, *The Gold Pan Mining Company and Shops*, from this rare collection.

Back in 1963, Jim had purchased their South Ridge Street home, a log cabin constructed as a fire department fund-raiser raffle item, and added on until it became a large and hospitable family residence. The two filled their home with antiques from Maureen's longtime store, Quandary Antiques, and mine artifacts from around Breckenridge. Jim gathered their white quartz fireplace rock from near the Peak 10 summit and the mantle beam came from the Ware Carpenter Smelter on Ski Hill Road.

Jim worked as a real estate broker. He purchased and remodeled the historic Charles A. Finding Hardware building into an office for his architecture-design business.

Jim and Maureen have poured themselves out in giving to Breckenridge. And Breckenridge, in turn, has opened its heart to give back to them. One twinge that pains the couple lies in growth. "We used to know everyone in town." Another lies in natural change, which has caused their older friends to leave. But they view growth with this philosophy, expressed by Maureen:

You have to accept and grow with it. It's fun to grow with the town. If you don't like it—and there are things I don't like—you have to accept it or leave.

The Nicholls, Jim and Maureen, long ago planted their feet in Breckenridge. They will never leave.

Heritage Sites to Intrigue Visitors

As it did decades ago, 1875-built Carter Museum delights adults and kids.

Stories from Breckenridge's past come alive with a tour of the town's dozen or more heritage sites. When history lovers step into a Victorian parlor, experience Edwin Carter's Museum or stroll past Main Street's log and clapboard buildings, they can imagine scenes from the past. Gentlemen with gold nugget watch chains and ladies in bustle skirts with parasols once enjoyed the same street scenes, mountain views and mining stories that heritage visitors enjoy today.

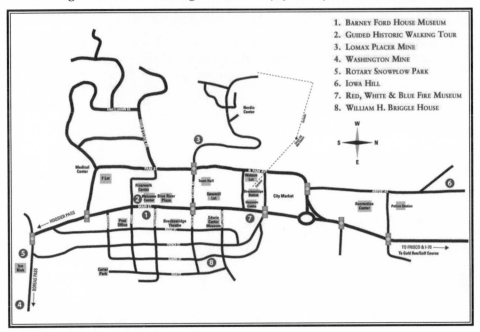

1. BARNEY FORD HOUSE MUSEUM
2. GUIDED HISTORIC WALKING TOUR
3. LOMAX PLACER MINE
4. WASHINGTON MINE
5. ROTARY SNOWPLOW PARK
6. IOWA HILL
7. RED, WHITE & BLUE FIRE MUSEUM
8. WILLIAM H. BRIGGLE HOUSE

Heritage Alliance Sites: easy to access by foot, bike, or car; some by town bus.

Detail, Barney Ford House

Breckenridge Heritage Alliance sites:

Barney Ford House Museum,
111 East Washington

Edwin Carter Museum,
111 North Ridge

William H. Briggle House,
104 North Harris

Milne and Eberlein houses,
Milne Park next to Briggle House

Red, White and Blue Fire Museum,
316 North Main Street

Welcome Center and Museum, Blue River Plaza, Main Street at Washington

Washington Mine Interpretive Site, Illinois

Gulch, Road 518 off Boreas
Pass Road

Lomax Placer Mine Intrepre-
tive Site, Lomax Gulch, 0.4
mile west up Ski Hill Road

Rotary Snowplow Park, Boreas
Pass Road next to Ice Rink

Reiling Dredge, 2.7 miles east
on French Gulch road, trail
at right

Iowa Hill Placer, Iowa Hill, Ari-
port Road just north of town
(left at sign)

Fuqua Stables

Town of Breckenridge and Other Sites:

Summit County Courthouse, 208 Lincoln

1908 schoolhouse, 103 South Harris

Country Boy Mine

Fuqua Livery Stable,
110 East Washington

Country Boy Mine,
542 County Road 565,
French Gulch

B & B Mines open space,
Swan and French Gulches

Mining History on Backcountry Trails

Breckenridge's Golden Horseshoe, an arc of the region's richest mining property northeast of town, became more user-friendly with a $9 million town-county land purchase in 2005. The B & B Mines buy made available to recreation users a bounty of hiking, mountain-biking and ski-snowshoe trails. Studded with historic treasures, the

1,840-acre alpine playground features mines, mine equipment and remains, dredges and historic ruins.

A wealth of history lies just to the east of Breckenridge in French Gulch, the location of dozens of early mining operations. In 2009, the Breckenridge Heritage Alliance has installed interpretive signage to highlight

B & B Mines open space still has mining relics.

the stories of mines that once thrived in the area. Historic photographs will show French Gulch visitors how the landscape has changed to its present appearance and bring alive a rich past.

The visitor-friendly project includes interpretive signage for 12 mining-interest areas:

1. Mekka Bedrock Flume, riches on the historic Sisler Placer (Wellington Road)
2. Extenuate (X10U8) Trailhead, crucible of Breckenridge's most famous mine
3. Rose of Breckenridge Mine, golden dreams and dashed hopes
4. Minnie Mine, Traylor Shaft and Dredge Site, underground and streambed mining
5. Truax Mine Lower Tunnel, hardrock mining adit
6. Truax Mine, Upper Tunnel, lead, silver and gold
7. Minnie Trailhead, a hike into mine history
8. Lucky Mine and Mill, investment ruined by the 1893 silver crash
9. Dredge Tailings Piles, rich yield, environmental bust
10. Reiling Dredge, a 1900s money-maker
11. Exploration Shaft, a dangerous "coyote" burrow?
12. Depression-era Mining, jerry-rigged equipment from grim years

Whether its an in-town, hands-on heritage experience or an adventure in the mine-rich backcountry, Breckenridge still resonates with its historic past. One-hundred and fifty years lay behind. Many years of exploring its gold rush past lie ahead.

Index

Photo Credits

The author gratefully acknowledges the following individuals and organizations for allowing use of these photographs:

Cover photograph, Carl Scofield. Back cover, inside front and inside back cover photographs, Mary Ellen Gilliland. Contents Page: Jim Yust. All etchings from *Harpers Illustrated Weekly,* unless indicated otherwise below.

Page: 10 National Geographic Topo! Colorado; 23 Bill Fountain; 28 Author's Collection; 34 Alabama Department of Archives and State History, Montgomery, Alabama; 36 Author's Collection; 37 Denver Public Library; 40 Archives & Special Collections, Mansfield Library, University of Montana; 42 *Mining Journal,* 1877; 43 Author's Collection; 44 National Geographic Topo! Colorado; 45 Chamberlain photo from Bill Fountain; 49 Bill Fountain; 50 Mary Ellen Gilliland; 52 Ed and Nancy Bathke Collection; 53 and 55 Mary Ellen Gilliland; 58 Summit County Clerk and Recorder-Bill Fountain; 60 Inset: Summit Historical Society postcard; Photo: Author's Collection; 64 Mary Ellen Gilliland; 65 1880s Summit County Government document art; 67 and 68 Author's Collection; 69 and 70 Ed and Nancy Bathke Collection; 71 Jim Yust; 72 Denver Public Library; 73 Summit Historical Society; 75 Glenn Campbell; 76 and 77 Author's Collection; 78 Summit Historical Society; 81a and b Author's Collection; 82 Denver Public Library; 84 Ed and Nancy Bathke Collection; 85 Jim Yust; 86 Mary Ellen Gilliland; 87 *Summit County Journal;* 88 Colorado Springs Ghost Town Club; 89 Author's Collection; 90 Jim Yust; 92 Denver Public Library; 95 Ed and Nancy Bathke Collection; 96 Author Collection; 97 and 98 Jim Yust; 101 *Summit County Journal;* 102 Mary Ellen Gilliland; 103, 104 and 106 Roxie Kaiser Knudsen;107 Jim Yust; 108 Author's Collection; 109 Denver Public Library; 110, 112 and 115 Author's Collection; 117 Virginia Brown Kloberdanz; 119 and 120 Denver Public Library; 121 Author's Collection; 123 Wendy Wolfe; 125 Cynthia Peabody Anderson; 128 Denver Public Library; 129 Summit Historical Society; 131 Wendy Wolfe; 134 Maureen Nicholls; 137 Mary Ellen Gilliland; 138a Breckenridge Heritage Alliance; 138b, 139a and b, 140 Mary Ellen Gilliland

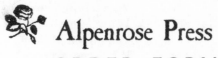

Alpenrose Press

ORDER FORM

Please mail my book(s) to me at this address:

Name:

Address: _____

City: _____ State: _____ ZIP:

___(Quantity)   BRECKENRIDGE   17.95 ea.
                                          Colorado only tax 0.52

___(Quantity)   The New Summit Hiker   17.95 ea.
                                          Colorado only tax 0.52

___(Quantity)   The Vail Hiker   17.95 ea.
                                          Colorado only tax 0.52

___(Quantity)   SUMMIT softcover   24.95 ea.
                                          Colorado only tax 0.72

___(Quantity)   SUMMIT hardcover   33.95 ea.
                                          Colorado only tax 0.98

___(Quantity)   Rascals, Scoundrels & No Goods   19.95 ea.
                                          Colorado only tax 0.58

       Postage & Handling @ 3.50 ea. book   _____
       (**Free** Postage on 3 or more books!)

Total Enclosed   _____

Check or Money Order Only

Send to: Alpenrose Press, Box 499, Silverthorne, CO 80498-0499

Request Free Author Autograph!

Please autograph my copy. To: _____
                                       (Name of Recipient)